THE FATE OF
ZIONISM

❖-❖-❖-❖-❖-❖-❖

THE FATE OF
ZIONISM

❖◇❖◇❖◇❖◇❖

A SECULAR FUTURE FOR
ISRAEL & PALESTINE

❖◇❖◇❖◇❖◇❖

ARTHUR HERTZBERG

HarperSanFrancisco
A Division of HarperCollins*Publishers*

HarperCollins books may be purchased for educational, business, or sales promotional use. For information please write: Special Markets Department, HarperCollins Publishers, Inc., 10 East 53rd Street, New York, NY 10022.

HarperCollins Web site: http://www.harpercollins.com
HarperCollins®, ■®, and HarperSanFrancisco™ are
trademarks of HarperCollins Publishers, Inc.

FIRST EDITION
Designed by Joseph Rutt

Library of Congress Cataloging-in-Publication Data available on request.
ISBN 0-06-0557869
03 04 05 06 07 RRD(H) 10 9 8 7 6 5 4 3 2 1

For
Edgar Bronfman and Jan Aronson
with abiding affection

CONTENTS

◇◇◇◇◇◇◇◇◇

INTRODUCTION

◇◇◇◇◇◇◇◇◇

In the last days of June 1967, I attended a meeting at Beit Berl, the conference center of the Labor Party, which had led modern Israel since it had begun seven decades before in the Zionist settlements in Palestine. Just weeks before, in six days of war between June 5 and 10, Israel had survived what had seemed to be a threat of annihilation by the Arab armies on all its borders. At the meeting at Beit Berl, American and Israeli Jews were celebrating, together, a victory of which we could not even have dreamt a few weeks ago. The armed forces of Israel had decisively conquered all of its enemies; Israel's rule suddenly extended to the Jordan River in the east and over the Sinai Peninsula in the south.

One could now fly to Mount Sinai or drive the short route from Jerusalem to the Sea of Galilee through what had been, just a few days before, the West Bank of Jordan. The *suq*, the market in the Old City of Jerusalem, was jammed with Jews. One could walk through the *suq* to the Western Wall, the retaining wall of the Second Temple, the only part of the shrine that had remained standing after its destruction by the Romans in the year 70. Jews had had no access to this site for the past twenty years. Soldiers in Israeli uniform were now guarding the Church of the Holy Sepulchre, the central holy place of Christianity, and the Temple Mount, on which two of the most sacred Muslim mosques had been erected thirteen centuries ago.

Those of us who came to that meeting in Beit Berl expected that we would be singing a historic song of victory—but we were mistaken. The principal event was the appearance of the most heroic figure in Israel, the one whom everyone agreed was larger than life, David Ben-Gurion. By 1967 he had left politics and moved to a kibbutz in the northern edge of Israel's desert. He was spending his days writing, receiving visitors, and sending out occasional thunderbolts, so that Israel and the world would remember that he had not become a helpless god.

Ben-Gurion arrived late that night. He came dressed in the shorts that befitted a member of a kibbutz, and he was clearly in bad humor. I happened to be speaking when he arrived, and I soon got a note from the chairman of the evening informing me that I had already gone over my time limit as the "warm-up" for Ben-Gurion. He had made it clear that if I did not relinquish the platform to him within the next five minutes, he would just get up and leave. Of course I complied and sat down to listen to the "George Washington of Israel." He surprised everyone in that room. Ben-Gurion, the brave statesman and undaunted military leader who had won Israel's war for its independence, asserted that if Israel did not now give back, immediately, all the territory that it had captured in recent days—with the exception of East Jerusalem—it would be heading for historic disaster.

In that room that day, no one believed him at all except me. I could not simply write off what he had said as the anger of an old man who could not accept that he had become irrelevant. I knew that as a person he could be petty and angry, but not on issues of great historic importance. What I heard him say kept gnawing at me. What if he was right?

It took me a couple of years of hard thinking to become one of Ben-Gurion's followers. And it has taken some thirty more years of involvement in the politics of the Middle East for me to know beyond any shadow of a doubt that the aging, worried, and even bitter Ben-Gurion was the true Zionist prophet in June 1967. He saw that the Zionism he had helped fashion in the early years of the twentieth century, a movement whose main goal was the creation and support of a Jewish national state in Palestine, was being overlaid after June 1967 with Israeli triumphalism and myths about the advent of a messianic age. Zionism required a return to its first principles. After three decades of reflection on my last encounter with David Ben-Gurion, I now understand why he so passionately denied the seeming glories of that great victory in June 1967. He was afraid that Zionism, for which he had suffered and dared, was being replaced by a new—and false—religion.

With the last of his strength, he was uttering a solemn warning against the delusions of power. Yes, Israel could not survive without power in its own hands. David Ben-Gurion knew better than anyone what the central meaning of modern Zionism was: the Jewish people could no longer endure as an embattled minority; they needed the power to make their own destiny. But the result of the Six-Day War, earlier in the month of June 1967, was that Jewish power was now overextended. The recent conquests were evoking dreams of grandeur that might be realized if the messiah were indeed about to appear; but Ben-Gurion had come to Palestine in the aftermath of pogroms in eastern Europe, and he had led the Yishuv, the Zionist settlement, in the early 1940s while it lived in terror that Hitler's armies might succeed in invading Palestine and destroying its Jews along with the millions whom Hitler was murdering in Europe. The messiah had not come in the first five decades of the twentieth century when he should have been sent to save Jews. Ben-Gurion did not believe that he might appear now to safeguard Jewish possession of the Sinai Peninsula, or even of the West Bank, the biblical Judea and Samaria.

The morning after Ben-Gurion's speech I left the meeting to drive to Jerusalem. The mood of the city was jubilant. That very day I visited all the places that had been forbidden to Jews since 1948. I went to the Western Wall but also to the oldest Jewish cemetery, which had existed for almost three thousand years on the Mount of Olives, and I even had coffee at the end of this heady tour on the veranda of the Intercontinental Hotel. What a victory it was to look out toward the Temple Mount and see the golden glow of the Dome of the Rock (commonly called the Mosque of Omar)—from the east, from the Arab side. But David Ben-Gurion had planted in me a recurrent discomfort. It was the question Is this what Zionism means? Do we want to be a triumphant people or will it be enough for us to become a people of peace with each other and with our neighbors? How much power do the Jewish people need in order to achieve their ultimate ambitions for themselves?

Ben-Gurion had asked nothing less than the fundamental question What had the Zionists come to the land of Palestine to accomplish? He was very clear that the conquest of extended territories was no better than the quest for power that had animated innumerable conquerors everywhere throughout history. Jews had a right to be in Palestine only if they had come in the name of honorable purposes, not so they could succumb to intoxication with a great victory. We had to know why Jews had wound up on this firing line. We even had to know why so many Arabs, both in Palestine and elsewhere, had opposed Zionism and gone to war against it and yet be able to say to them in good conscience that we had not come to conquer them.

Now, thirty-five years after this unforgettable encounter with David Ben-Gurion, Zionism and the state of Israel are again targets. I feel constrained to explain myself as a Zionist and to define my passion for the state of Israel. I have learned to follow after David Ben-Gurion, who dissented, at the end of his life, from the platform of the very Labor Party he had helped to fashion and who was critical of programs of the Israeli government even when it was run by politicians who proclaimed themselves his disciples. In this book, I shall be making the case for Zionism, not as a Zionist zealot or even as a critical adherent, but as a disciple of the founders of the movement. I shall look through their eyes at their vision of themselves and at the fundamental question they faced again and again: How could they make peace with the Arabs?

ONE

BACK TO THE FUTURE

Ben-Gurion's instincts in June 1967 were very much on target. The "new" Zionism that he warned about was a secular movement, but it had never quite broken its connection with the Jewish religion. After the Six-Day War many Zionists believed that this great victory was proof that God was on their side. They were all the more certain that they were special people and living at a special time because the Jews now had more power than they had ever before possessed. The favor of God and their own military strength guaranteed their future. But these notions were and remain a delusion. Modern Zionism can succeed today only if it emphasizes its largely secular origins. It dare not walk down the path of religious certainty or the arrogance of power.

WHAT IS ZIONISM?

The short definition of modern Zionism is that it is a political movement for a Jewish national state in Palestine begun by Austrian journalist Theodor Herzl. Herzl insisted that the Jews had to become a "normal people" in a land of their own. Otherwise, the "abnormality" of the Jews as a beleaguered minority everywhere would persist. We will be going into much greater detail later in the chapter, but readers may get a better idea of what modern Zionism consists of by first considering what it excludes or even denies. Modern Zionism did not arise to carry out an imperative of the Jewish faith that God had designated the Holy Land as the ultimate home of the Jews. The Jewish religious imperative had always been defined as forbidding the Jews to take direct action themselves to re-create their kingdom; their return had to wait for God's miraculous intervention. Indeed, from the very beginning to this day, the majority of Orthodox Jews of the world have not accepted Zionist ideology, which does advocate human endeavor on behalf of the establishment of a Jewish national state. The movement that Herzl launched side-stepped the inherited Jewish faith to propose that not faith in God but rallying against anti-Semitism was the tie that bound Jews together. His critics among the Zionists found him to be too assimilated (in December he had a Christmas tree in his apartment in Vienna), but they too were overwhelmingly secular; they wanted to redo Judaism and make of it a national culture in Hebrew. To this day the cultural capital of Zionism remains Tel Aviv, the most secular of Israeli cities, and not Jerusalem, which is very nearly dominated by Orthodox believers.

It is of the most profound importance that modern Zionism not be identified as the lineal heir to the religion of the Bible. If the Jewish claim to a homeland in Palestine rests on the assertion that it is the Holy Land that God promised to Abraham for his children, it follows that Muslims have the right to claim that the Prophet made the site of the ancient temple holy to the new Islamic faith through the miracle of arriving there one night from Medina and immediately ascending from there to heaven. It can be argued, further, that the land as a whole belongs to followers of the Prophet because they conquered it soon after the faith of Islam was proclaimed; it is a doctrine of Islam that all such lands are forever inalienable. By the same token, Christians have long maintained that the Jews can return to the Holy Land only as part of the miracle of the end of days, which will happen as part of the second coming of Christ. This age will begin with the acceptance by the Jews en masse of faith in Jesus. Obviously, these three religious scenarios are incompatible, and they cannot compromise. Followers of each faith might agree to wait for the end of days to find out which of these religious dramas is correct, but they would have to agree that actual arrangements in the Holy Land today can only be pragmatic, essentially secular, and based on considerations other than predictions that stem from literalist readings of various religious texts.

It is even more important within the Jewish community that modern Zionism not be identified as the heir and continuation of the messianic element in classic Jewish religion. If the Zionist endeavor is ever dominated by the notion that Jews have come back to Palestine as a giant step toward the coming of the messiah, there can be no peace within the Jewish camp. Such messianists are sure that they are carrying out the will of God. They can—indeed, they must—disregard

Israeli governments that have put limits on or even tried to stop the actions of settlers in the West Bank. Some of these believers encouraged the assassination of a prime minister of Israel, Yitzhak Rabin. The assassin himself acted in good conscience; he was removing someone who was willing to give back to the Arabs most, or perhaps all, of the land of the West Bank. Thus, Rabin had, so the messianists insisted, put himself beyond the pale by having become an enemy of God.

This religious absolutism leads to the further conclusion that aggressive Jewish endeavors on its behalf do not have to make any rational political sense. Thus, a small but vehement group exists in contemporary Israel that calls itself Ateret Kohanim. Some members have been stopped several times from putting dynamite under the foundations on which the Dome of the Rock stands; it had been built where the inner sanctuary of the Jewish Temple in Jerusalem once stood. Fortunately such attempts were aborted by the Israeli police, but members of Ateret Kohanim have never given up their certainty that this act of clearing the Temple Mount should be carried out; success in dynamiting the Dome of the Rock will evoke divine help in the immediate restoration of the Holy Temple in Jerusalem. Some associated with this group have been weaving garments for the priests who will serve in this temple and making vessels, as described in the Bible, to be used in the sacred services that will soon begin. It is of course obvious, even to these enthusiasts, that if they ever succeed in destroying the Dome of the Rock, what will follow, rationally speaking, is an unimaginably bitter war of religion. But this doesn't worry many of the new messianists. They feel free to engage in the most dangerous provocations because they are certain that they will be forcing God to come down to earth and give them victory.

Unfortunately, these messianists do not seem to have a long historical memory. Nineteen centuries ago armed Zealots forced a revolt against the Roman masters of the land, despite the hesitancy of the most important religious leader of the day, Johanan ben Zakkai. He counseled patience and moderation and insisted that with the difference in power between the Roman legions and the Jewish revolutionaries there could be no victory for a Jewish revolt. Johanan ben Zakkai taught that the highest act of virtue was to establish peace "between nation and nation, between government and government, between family and family."[1] The Zealots responded that God himself could not let their cause fail. He would not let the Holy Temple fall into the hands of the Roman idolaters. The revolt held out for three years but, as Johanan ben Zakkai had foreseen, it failed. He knew that the hand of God could not be forced. Today, messianic madness has seized one element of the Jewish people. Its members are small in number, but their passion and activism appeal beyond the community of the faithful. This messianism reinforces among some Jews the feeling that, by exercising power unashamedly, they are not candidates for another Holocaust.

THE SIX-DAY WAR BRINGS A RADICAL CHANGE IN ZIONISM

It is not difficult to understand why some Jews have turned in recent decades to such activist messianism. After the

Six-Day War in June 1967, the mass mood of the Jews in Israel and elsewhere in the world was euphoric. A miracle had taken place. So why could this miracle not be the harbinger of others on the way to realizing the age-old messianic dreams of the Jews? The trouble with this messianism is that it had long been forbidden in the Talmud itself. The Jewish people had been warned that they should not try to predict the time of their redemption, because that was a mystery known only to God; nor should they engage in any active endeavors, and certainly not in the use of arms, to force "the end of days."

I lived through the aftermath of the Six-Day War, and I was enveloped by the messianic enthusiasm that was felt even by some seemingly secular Jews. I could not share it. On the contrary, I kept saying, first to myself and then ever more publicly and insistently, that if the Jewish messiah had chosen the twentieth century as the time to appear, he should have come to Auschwitz or to Lvov, where my grandfather and all my mother's siblings and their families were being murdered. I cannot believe that Jews can defy logic in Israel and presume that the messiah will come to save them from the political and military debts they are running up in order to expand the settlements of the West Bank.

These reflections lead inevitably to the most fundamental consideration of all: What indeed is the state of Israel in the minds of the Jews? When it was first created in 1948, the official rabbinate of Israel wrote a prayer in which Israel was described as "the first flowering of our redemption." This phrase was not taken with any profound literal seriousness at the time even among religious believers. The dominant theology among the religious moderates—a minority of perhaps 10 percent of Israel's population in those early days—was to wait for the miraculous events that had been foretold in the religious tradition. Their dreams would be realized in some future time, when God willed it.

But after 1967 the crucial phrase in the prayer—"the first flowering of our redemption"—acquired a new meaning. Israel was now imagined as a sacred enterprise that was revealing its true intent and purpose. Never mind that the Zionist movement had begun among secular Jews with avowed purposes that had little or nothing to do with the inherited religious tradition or were even hostile to it. God had supposedly used the secular pioneers who had created the agricultural settlements—and the antireligious nationalists who were the creators of modern Hebrew as a language—as the instrument of his will. His redemption of the Jews was now under way.

This new vision of modern Zionism was profoundly revolutionary. It had been defined in the early years of the twentieth century by a great rabbinic scholar who was also a mystic and a kabbalist, Rabbi Abraham Isaac Kook. He had come to Palestine in 1904 when he was elected to be the rabbi of the Jewish community in Jaffa, which was then the center of Zionist endeavor and the port of entry for Jewish immigrants. Soon after Great Britain was given the mandate by the League of Nations to govern Palestine, the Jews were empowered, in 1922, to create a legally recognized national authority for themselves. This body unhesitatingly chose Rabbi Kook to be the chief rabbi of the Holy Land.

Kook found the way to unite all the disparate and often clashing elements of the Zionist community: he portrayed them as part of the same people. They were one, far more deeply than they could possibly know. Kook's Zionist vision made it possible for him to love all Jews, even those with whom he disagreed, even if they proclaimed that they hated God. God was writing straight—that is, he was bringing redemption now, in our own day. Each of the lines God was writing seemed to be random and even crooked, but together they defined the straight path to the end of days.

Rabbi Abraham Isaac Kook was almost universally acknowledged to be a holy man whose heart was full of love and hope. He never translated his messianic dreams into the justification to do battle with those who disagreed with him. But a messianic doctrine always contains within it the possibility, even the probability, of anger directed against the enemies of God. What if the messiah tarries? If he does not come soon, as Kook wanted, who is to blame? The most obvious answer is that people who do not believe in him have stood in the way of his coming. Kook himself never arrived at this complaint, but his son, Rabbi Zvi Yehuda Kook, did reach this second phase of anger and recrimination.

Together with his brother-in-law, Shalom Nathan-Raanan, Zvi Yehuda had inherited from his father, who died in 1935, the leadership of the *yeshiva* (school of Talmudic studies) that his father had founded. Zvi Yehuda Kook was certain—and he taught his students to be certain—that God had promised to the Jews the undivided land of Israel and that this promise would soon be kept. Anyone who stood in the way of the realization of this promise had to be pushed aside. This was the younger Kook's view even before the great victories in the Six-Day War, but he was certain of it after that "miracle." What his father had predicted was now happening before the eyes of the world: the Jews were in control of all the land of Israel and much more beside, including even Mount Sinai itself. These gains had to be the last step on the way to messianic redemption. Those who followed Zvi Yehuda Kook could now disregard what modern Zionism had done, or thought that it had done. He and his followers understood correctly the meaning and purpose of the return of the Jews to the land. It was indeed "the first flowering of our redemption." The time was now.

It does not require much analysis or profound insight today to see that messianism, in all its grandeur and grandiosity, was and remains the path toward interminable bitter battles with those who feel buffeted by this Jewish claim. It has led to unceasing internal strife within the Jewish community. These ideas have been and continue to be advanced with great fervor by some elements in Israel and in the Jewish world as a whole, but they have never swept aside the more sober and pragmatic self-definitions of the founders of modern Zionism.

So, to return to the question that I posed at the beginning of this discussion, How did modern Zionism define itself? Are these definitions still valid? Are they more valid than the flamboyant and warlike new Zionism of messianic faith and the assertion of Jewish power?

MODERN ZIONISM REDEFINES THE JEWS

Modern Zionism was created in the last years of the nineteenth century as a bulwark against anti-Semitism and Jewish homelessness. The Zionists proposed to create a national homeland where the Jews could solve, or at least alleviate, their basic problems in the modern age. They had acquired equality, on paper, in much of Europe, but they had been served up persecution during the eighty years after this new policy was proclaimed by the French Revolution: Jews had been promised access to the very heights of Western culture, but they were forced to remain semi-outsiders, looking in. Worst of all, many of these assimilating Jews no longer retained strong roots in the traditions of their own people. They had no spiritual home to which to return.

This conception of the state of Israel cast for it very pragmatic and immediate roles in the strengthening and safeguarding of the Jewish people. It made no grandiose plans for the ultimate future. Yes, even those sober Zionists often dreamt of a rosy rebirth of all of humanity into a radically new and better world by the agency of the representatives of Abraham, who had once proclaimed monotheism—but this was rhetoric and not a political program. Indeed, in his later years, in the 1970s and 1980s, Sir Isaiah Berlin, the most redoubtable Zionist among British intellectuals, kept insisting, quite provocatively, that his vision of the future of the state of Israel utterly denied the dream of its being a "light unto the nations." It was enough that the Zionist revolution achieve its real purpose: to make of the Jews a normal people.

Berlin used to add with a flourish that it would be enough if Israel became another Albania. I never quite believed Isaiah Berlin really meant this, that he had no soft spot in his heart for the notion of a Jewish state that would breed intellectuals of world rank and Nobel Prize winners in the sciences, but he kept insisting that the reality of Zionism was much more modest. It wanted a secure place for Jews in the world, a place they knew that they would have to share with others; it was the place toward which the Balfour Declaration, the charter for the creation of a Jewish national home, had pointed.

Zionism must, of course, also be defended against the often slanderous attacks that keep being mounted nowadays with ever increasing vehemence by its critics and enemies on the left. Much of their distemper with Zionism is leveled at the doctrines and actions of the new Jewish messianists, but many of these critics have long been attacking the Zionist enterprise as a whole. They do not want to see that Zionism began and is still rooted in the very values that these critics themselves profess to espouse. Modern Zionism affirms the right of all peoples, including the Jews, to live under decent conditions, in security, and in relationships of respect and equality with other peoples. The whole point of the endeavor was to end the homelessness and the vulnerability of the Jews. Like all other peoples, Jews should have a homeland and not remain targets for their enemies. Is this not the liberal and universalist doctrine of the past century or two?

I am sure that if one could revive Theodor Herzl and his circle and speak with them, one would be in the presence of men and women who thought of themselves as trying to achieve for Jews what Giuseppe Mazzini was creating in the mid-nineteenth century for Italians and what the European revolutionaries of 1848 had wanted to create throughout much of the Continent. Why is it morally acceptable to be a vehement proponent of Palestinian nationalism, even when it expresses itself in immoral actions such as suicide bombings, and remain very cross with Jewish nationalism, especially when it expresses itself in sometimes excessive countermeasures? The issue of the present attacks on Zionism, and especially the question of how much these attacks are really nourished from ancient subterranean rivers of anti-Semitism in Europe, needs to be discussed, but at the moment let us understand what Zionism really is.

Modern Zionism, when it appeared, was a peculiar case. It offered to change the Jews into a contemporary secular nation, and thus it sounded as if it were responding to the demands of the leaders of modern society that Jews play by their rules. Thus, Zionism found adherents among some of the leaders of opinion in Western culture. But Zionism also contained a very strong demand for Jews to gather together to live by their own reworking of their inherited values and cultures. This divide, between the assimilationist demand that had been posed in the eighteenth century by the leaders of the Enlightenment and the drive of most Jews for a re-assertion of their own cultures and traditions, has been the deepest source of tension between Western intellectuals and Zionists. When Jews did anything that their critics did not like, it could be used against them: they were displaying their old ways—and their old ways of being themselves were, by "enlightened" definition, discredited. Thus, the door remained open to condemning Jews whenever they did not behave as some intellectuals thought they should.

Behind the criticism—in fact, its very premise—was the inherited certainty of some Western intellectuals that the Jews were really a problem people who, after the days of the Bible, had added nothing to Western society. It would be easy to score polemical points by listing the inconsistencies and moral failings of those who criticize Israel today. It is all too easy to prove that Western liberals keep sitting by quietly and doing nothing about far worse outrages than those they claim to see in Israel. The Palestinian case is fundamentally skewed by the use of terrorism against civilians and murder by suicide bombers. Nonetheless, we need to define Zionism itself—its intentions and its failures—to begin to understand the fundamental issues that are now being fought out and debated.

Modern Zionism began late in the nineteenth century with two fundamental and often contradictory visions of the Jewish people. One school of thought, led by the founder of political Zionism, the legendary Theodor Herzl, wanted to make of the Jews a "normal people": Herzl proposed to remake them into a secular nation living on its own land and governed by its own state, which he envisioned as fashioned by late-nineteenth-century ideas. He was concerned with the destiny of the Jews and especially the millions of Jews who were suffering persecution in eastern and central Europe. But most of those who readily became Zionists were not really his followers; they belonged to the second school of thought.

13

The second school's view had been defined by its principal spokesman, Asher Ginzberg, who wrote in Hebrew under the pen name Ahad Ha'am, "one of the people," but this intellectual was no ordinary person. He had a profound rabbinic education but turned in his twenties into a religious agnostic. Ahad Ha'am quickly became the principal spokesman of a movement that defined itself as cultural Zionism. He and his followers affirmed the history and memories of the Jewish people and substituted for the Orthodox religion the inherited Hebraic culture of the Jews. They wanted a Jewish state that would afford Jews the power to make whatever changes they needed in the forms and even the content of their tradition. For such Zionists the ultimate objective of the movement was not to acquire the national structures that would turn them into another ordinary small nation. They could not relinquish the self-image of the Jews as a unique people with a history of both suffering and creativity that, in their Jewish self-assessment, no other people ever matched.

The followers of Ahad Ha'am had no illusion, as Herzl did, that all the Jews who wanted to continue in that identity would soon be gathered into the "Jewish national home." They wanted to establish a modern cultural center that would radiate out its spirit to all Jews wherever they might be living. So, modern Zionism was defined at the end of the nineteenth century by Theodor Herzl's desire for a political Jewish state that would make of the Jews a "normal people" and by Ahad Ha'am's insistence that a renascent Jewish community in the land of the ancestors had to be a proud affirmation of the work and values of Jewish culture and spirit through the ages.

Ahad Ha'am called attention as early as the 1890s to the presence of Arabs in the land and predicted that the relationship between the new Jewish immigrants and the existing Arab population would be the most difficult and enduring problem in Palestine. This observer knew that the Arabs would not vanish from Palestine. He was proved right almost immediately. The first new Jewish farming settlements were being created at about the time he wrote, a few years before Theodor Herzl appeared on the scene to create political Zionism. The popular movement that called itself "Lovers of Zion" was bringing Jews who wanted to leave pogrom-ridden Russia to Palestine. Their farms were immediately attacked by marauders, who were very often Bedouins, but sometimes settled Arab neighbors. Jews had no choice but to guard their lives. When Jewish immigration increased after 1904, Jewish farmers had to organize a defense organization, Hashomer, which was the lineal ancestor of the Israeli defense forces of today. Ahad Ha'am was right; the die was being cast very early and a century of conflict was beginning. As we shall soon see, the main issues have remained remarkably stable—and intractable.

The Zionist movement therefore began with a deep tension, even a contradiction, at its very heart. It was asking itself to remake the Jewish people as a modern, Western entity, even as it was asking itself to remake the Jewish people so that in a new age it could still function as a "light unto the nations." Inevitably, it asked those who would help the

Zionist cause to blur this distinction. It was an issue that neither the Zionists nor those who looked at them from the outside could avoid. But the issue was not really unique to the Jews; it is the fundamental tension of all modern nationalisms, between the claim of universal rights and the desire for the right of self-determination, between the desire to belong to all of humanity and the devotion to specific identities. There is, for that matter, no version of modern social thought, from the most conservative to the most radical, that has not confronted and does not continue to wrestle with the question of what to do with a past of its own group, even as it is trying to navigate its way into a new, more spacious and useful future. What the Jews were asking through Zionism amounted to a plea that they too should be offered the chance to participate in the great international debate about the future of the many individual societies and cultures and the shape that their relations with one another should take.

REACTIONS TO ZIONISM

Before digging deeper, as we inevitably must, into the meaning of the tension between the universal and the particular at the heart of Zionism, it is profoundly important that we understand what the two aims of Zionism have evoked among both its non-Jewish supporters and its enemies. The supporters have tended to seize on the Herzlian vision of the disappearance of Judaism, that is, of Jewish cultural and spiritual particularism, into a universalist, enlightened society. Such people have been impatient and often angry with the kind of Zionism that emphasizes and strengthens Jewish otherness.

An important change in progressive thinking has taken place in recent years. In the late 1940s people who regarded themselves as decent and progressive were sympathetic to the Jews and tended to be supporters of Zionism. Richard Crossman, a leading British socialist and member of the Anglo-American Commission of 1946, went to Palestine for the first time just after World War II and was particularly impressed by the Jewish farming communes in the Galilee. He saw in this Zionist effort the realization of what he thought progressives all over the world should be doing in their own societies. Indeed, nearly a half century earlier, in the years before World War I, Louis Brandeis, who would soon become a justice of the Supreme Court in the United States, had justified his conversion to Zionism by seeing the renascent Jewish community in Palestine as the best realization in the world of the progressive ideals that were then very prominent in American politics. The Jewish settlements would be the incarnation of social justice and economic equality. When Brandeis dreamt this dream he felt supported by a somewhat earlier vision of Theodor Herzl himself. Herzl had designed a flag for the Zionist movement featuring seven stars. Herzl was not a socialist, but the seven stars represented an advanced version of consideration for the rights of labor. He proposed in the 1890s that, in the new Jewish homeland he hoped to create, the working day should be limited to seven hours.

But now, more than a half century after the Holocaust, it is possible for some leaders of left-wing opinion to be so hostile to Israel as to wish it were not there. Never mind that a number of Third World regimes have behaved murderously toward their opponents and especially against national and religious minorities. Granting that the Palestinians are indeed suffering, are they more entitled to our concern than those who have been gassed or shot by the tens of thousands in Saddam Hussein's Iraq?

One cannot escape the conclusion that the outcry about the suffering of the Palestinians expresses a not too well hidden pleasure at finding reason to bash the Jews. This unworthy emotion is evident in the present outcry in some quarters of American academic life. The political cause of choice last year (in 2002) was to demand that universities disinvest in any company that has anything to do with Israel. It is strange that these defenders of human rights have not asked that the stocks of several big oil companies that have been supporting the most murderous rebel militias in Africa be declared impure and untouchable. The vehement, selective attacks on Israel have about them some aroma of "give it to the Jews." It is especially revealing that whenever these attacks are challenged, the response has usually been not to argue the facts. Instead, the opponents of Zionism and Israel wrap themselves in the flags of morality ("We are the ones who speak for virtue") and free speech ("How dare you censor us?").

But the issue is not censorship—it is truth. Those who are attacking Zionism and Israel today cannot avoid a counterattack. They cannot erase the truths of the conflict by recourse to high-sounding rhetoric. To challenge the detractors of Zionism and of Israel is not to censor the self-proclaimed bearers of high-mindedness. It is to hold them to account. They must face this challenge to their intellectual and moral integrity.

TWO

✧✧✧✧✧✧✧✧

THE STALEMATE
OF LEGITIMACY

Chaim Weizmann, the Zionist leader who was president of the World Zionist Organization for many decades, once said that the insoluble difficulty of the Palestine-Israel problem is that this is not a conflict between right and wrong—it is a conflict between two rights. The Palestinians have been insisting for more than a hundred years that they are the legitimate owners of Palestine because they have been the overwhelming majority of its population for at least thirteen centuries. Possession confers legitimacy. The Jews have maintained that they never lost connection with the land and have always regarded themselves exiles. The whole of Jewish culture is suffused with memory and longing for the land. Thus, the Jews' desire to return to the land has always existed as a central motif of Jewish experience. These competing claims for legitimacy have become ever more embittered, especially since the Jews began the Zionist venture by defining themselves as a persecuted minority, doubly endangered because assimilation was destroying the morale of the Jewish intelligentsia. On their side, the Palestinians have kept insisting that they are the permanent victims in this struggle, if only because they have no victories in which to rejoice as they contemplate the history of their struggle with the Jews.

Not far beneath the surface of both positions is a substratum of religion. Many Jews may say that they do not believe in God, but emotionally they act as if he had appeared in Palestine and had given the Jews back their ancient sovereignty. However, most Palestinians continue to believe the old Muslim doctrine that any land that was once possessed by the followers of Muhammad is inalienable; some of it may have been taken away by Crusaders in the Middle Ages or by Jewish settlers in modern times, but the land remains Muslim. As long as these contrasting assertions form the deep undertow of the Jewish-Arab encounter in Palestine, there can only be war. If there is ever to be a road to peace, the conflict must be secularized.

It is of the utmost importance to understand that the present quarrels are not new. The Jewish-Arab war—or, if you will, the Israeli-Palestinian war—is now more than a century old. Not only have the essential issues remained the same, but the rhetoric in which they are expressed has not really changed from the beginning.

As early as 1898, a Syrian, Christian-owned journal based in Cairo, *al Muqtataf,* published an article warning against Jewish hopes of controlling trade in Palestine. The next year Yusuf al-Khalidi, a prominent politician and intellectual, wrote to the chief rabbi in France, telling him that, although "historically it is your country" and Zionism could be understood in theory, in practice its implementation would require "brute force," and he pleaded with the rabbi to "let Palestine be left in peace."[1] Almost a century later, in the early 1990s, I shared a platform at a meeting in the Washington Cathedral with Walid Khalidi, a professor at Harvard and one of the most respected Palestinian intellectuals, to present our varying views on the Jewish-Arab conflict. Khalidi restated the essential Arab position with humor and brilliance: he admitted that he was prepared to believe that God had once promised the Jews the Holy Land, speaking to them in Hebrew, but he had never heard Allah saying the same in Arabic! I responded that we could alleviate the quarrel only if we laid aside religious absolutes, everyone's religious absolutes, and tried to find the most decent solution to the immediate problems between the two peoples, each of which claimed the land.

The terms of the quarrel were clear when it began, and thus I must ask a question. Why did so many decent people hail Zionism when it first appeared? The answer that comes trippingly to the tongues and pens of Zionism's detractors is to summon up the dread word "colonialism." Those who were for Zionism, especially the world powers, led by Great Britain, which helped to foster the role of the Zionists in Palestine, are now portrayed as being simply oblivious to the Arabs in the land. Worse still, the Jews in flight from pogroms and persecutions are described as coming to Palestine, not for refuge, but as colonialist conquerors. But is this true?

Political motives are, of course, varied and complex. When the British and the French divided power in the Middle East at the end of World War I, they had their own interests in mind. Both powers, but especially Great Britain, which received the mandate to govern Palestine, knew that they would have to do something substantial for the Jews, but not because this was an advantage for their colonial needs. Colonial interests would have favored the Arabs. They had the numbers and they populated the region. The British knew that the Arabs would not forgive them for whatever they were doing for the Zionists. They were not surprised that the Arabs sat on their hands during World War II, as many thought they could get a better deal for their national aspirations from the Nazis. Nonetheless, the British allowed, and often even helped, the Zionist movement to grow during much of the first half of the twentieth century.

The growth of Zionism in those decades was not an act of cold-blooded colonialism. At root, from the very beginning of its entry onto the international scene, modern Zionism was a matter of conscience. In the starkest terms, the rulers of the world were being asked, Can you look on with equanimity while the Jewish people are attacked en masse by anti-Semites and assimilated out of their own ethos by the various dominant cultures? Of course, even as many Western states accepted these arguments, they inevitably had in mind that their own populations were generally unfriendly or even hostile to the increasing influx of Jews from eastern Europe. Would it not be better to accept the Zionist vision of a secure home of their own for Jews? In the somewhat more decent decades before the Nazi era in the 1930s, the world answered yes—yes, in full awareness that the Arabs of Palestine and those who helped them were in armed rebellion. This was the moral calculus that led to the creation of the state of Israel. Let us examine why decisions were made to help the Jews. It then would be useful to ask an additional question: So what is different today?

BRITISH RESPONSES TO ZIONISM

A most revealing event happened in the very first years of the existence of modern Zionism. In 1903 the British government formally proposed to Theodor Herzl that his movement undertake to colonize a tract of land in Uganda, in an area that is now part of Kenya. Herzl wanted to accept the offer because of the dire condition of Jewish need. This was no substitute for Jewish settlement in the land of the ancestors, but it could act as a sorely needed "asylum for the night." Jews on the run from the relentless pogroms in Russia would at least find some refuge. Herzl was bitterly opposed within the Zionist movement by those who would accept not even a temporary substitute for the ancestral home in Palestine. At the Zionist Congress in August 1903, Herzl managed to convince the majority to agree to at least explore the question, but the Uganda proposal was essentially stopped by the divisive debate. It was abandoned soon after the death of Herzl in July 1904. Nonetheless, the fact that this proposal was made by the great empire of the day, Great Britain, to the nascent Zionist movement gave the Zionists diplomatic recognition. The offer of Uganda was thus the true beginning of the career of Zionism in international diplomacy.

Why did the British make the offer? They had had some previous dealings with Theodor Herzl over a change in their policy toward Jews in flight from Russia. In 1902 a committee of the British Parliament had called him to London to consult on where the Jewish refugees who were then leaving Russia en masse were supposed to go. Herzl, of course, did suggest that these fleeing masses should be directed to Palestine, but that could be done only with the assent of the Turkish rulers of the land, and they were not eager to receive many Jews.

Herzl did, however, succeed in convincing the parliamentary committee, and especially Lord Balfour, who was then the prime minister, that the Jews' need for personal security had become a world problem. In the first years of the twentieth century at least two million Jews were on the move, mostly to the United States, but some of them were coming to western Europe and to England, and a small number were somehow getting into Palestine. Herzl, the Zionist, had seized on a great contemporary problem: What was the world to do with this people in dire need? A year later, Herzl had elicited a response, the abortive offer of land in Uganda. The British did not need a new population in Uganda, but they seemed to think that a stretch of that land could be made habitable for Jews who needed to start their lives over again.

Zionism was given far greater status when it was recognized, during World War I, as a valid and serious national movement in international diplomacy by a declaration of the British government on November 2, 1917:

His Majesty's Government view with favour the establishment in Palestine of a national home for the
Jewish people, and will use their best endeavours to
facilitate the achievement of this object, it being
clearly understood that nothing shall be done which
may prejudice the civil and religious rights of existing non-Jewish communities in Palestine, or the
rights and political status enjoyed by Jews in any
other country.

The language of this declaration, the Balfour Declaration, had been fought over for months, phrase by phrase, so
that nothing accidental or merely rhetorical appears in its
text. In this declaration the British War Cabinet was affirm-
ing two principles, neither of which could be allowed to proceed to its own extreme. The Jews, who were then a small
minority in Palestine, some fifty thousand at most, were
given the right to establish a national home in Palestine and,
in effect, to be the leading force in the future of the country.
This right was conferred not primarily on the handful of Jews
in residence in Palestine; it was given to the Jewish people as
a whole, for which a Jewish agency would act. The World
Zionist Organization was immediately recognized as this
body. But what the Jews had gained did not include dominance over the Arab residents in the land. The questions of
how the Arab community would be governed and what role it
would play in making decisions for all of Palestine were left
undefined, but such rights were not abolished. The Balfour
Declaration told both Jews and Arabs alike that they would
have to live with a new situation that neither wanted.

Soon after the end of World War I, the peace conference that was held at Versailles in 1919 accepted the vision for the future of Palestine that Great Britain had announced in the Balfour Declaration. This agreement was finally enshrined in the peace treaty signed at San Remo in 1920, in which the very text of the Balfour Declaration was included as the foundation of the political order of the future in Palestine. The only state that exists now in a form rooted in the peace treaty after World War I is contemporary Israel. Jews like to think that this has happened because of the heroism of those who came to settle in the land and to create a new Jewish community and, ultimately, a Jewish state.

THE ARABS REJECT ZIONISM, AGAIN AND AGAIN

In Palestine itself, all this diplomacy had immediate results. The Jews accepted the Balfour Declaration and agreed to work under the mandate given to Great Britain to govern Palestine until it was ready for self-government, but the Arabs rejected it. They did what they had done before, and what they would do again and again in years to come: they went to war against the Jewish presence in Palestine in order to discourage more Jews from coming. In 1921 the Palestinian Arabs attacked various Jewish communities in the land and killed forty-seven Jews (forty-eight Arabs died as well).

Of course, not all Jews agreed, upon establishment of the British mandate for Palestine, that they would really be content with a Jewish national home, whatever that might be, since it was far less than what many Jews desired: that the Jewish people acquire sovereignty in all of Palestine, or at least in that part located west of the Jordan River. Nonetheless, mainstream Zionists and the majority of the Jewish people as a whole were willing to live under the terms of the Balfour Declaration and the British mandate. The Jews hoped that their activities would create a Jewish national home that would ultimately become a majority in Palestine through continued immigration and natural demographic increase.

Very few Jews ever doubted that the Arab population of Palestine would remain substantial and that Jews would have to treat Arabs with serious respect. The Zionists who were coming to Palestine in the 1920s and 1930s could simply not imagine that Arab hostility would be unrelieved and unrelenting. Eventually, so they thought, the anger of the Arabs of Palestine would cool and they would move toward some form of accommodation with the Jews. Elements of such accommodation did indeed occur through the years, but they kept being overwhelmed by those forces within the Palestinian community and the Arab world as a whole that refused to accept the presence of a significant Jewish national community in Palestine.

In the years before World War I, Arab-Jewish relations, especially in the cities where most Jews lived, did develop well in the realm of business. This was even true in the rural areas, where some Jewish farmers offered Arab labor relatively high wages. Nonetheless the underlying tensions remained. Every one of the Jewish colonies was occasionally attacked. Farther up the scale, the *effendis,* the dominant leaders among the Arabs in Palestine, had never shared political power with anyone else (except, of course, their Ottoman rulers). In 1920 a British Foreign Office booklet summarized the situation:

> There is . . . very widespread fear among Moslem land-owners that the program of Zionism is inimical to their interests; and societies have been formed to organize resistance to the sale of land to Jews.[2]

This description was reiterated in 1937 by the report of the Peel Commission:

> Willingness to co-operate with the Jews in municipal government is unhappily no evidence at all of willingness to co-operate on a national scale: and Arab councilors, who can agree with Jews about improving an urban-supply or regulating a market or laying out a park, cannot agree with them about the rate of immigration or land-purchase or the constitution of a Legislative Council. Practically all the Arab mayors, it will be remembered, attended the nationalist meeting at Jaffa which preceded the outbreak of 1933. And of course, the moderates among the Arab politicians have always made common cause with the extremists on major national issues.[3]

The story of Jewish purchase of Arab land does not always bear out the claim that there was large Arab unity in the face of Zionist expansion. On the contrary, there were enough landlords who were willing to sell land to the Jews. These purchases created grievances among the sharecroppers, who had cultivated a specific piece of soil for years and even generations. They were dispossessed and had to go find work elsewhere. Jewish accounts tended to minimize the numbers who were dispossessed; Arab accounts described them as "many thousands." The reality was that the numbers did not matter, though they were probably in between the minimalist account of some hundreds and the maximalist assertion of many thousands. What mattered was the attitudes of those who were arguing about the wrongs that supposedly had been done. It was in the interest of the Jews to minimize the injury to the Arabs; it was in the interest of the Arabs to proclaim how badly their people felt the hurt.

The most painful part of the story concerned the men and women of the "Second Aliyah," the second wave of Zionist immigrants, the young people who came in the early twentieth century and reflected the zest of the new Zionist movement. They believed passionately in the "conquest of work," that is, that Jews should do every job, including the most menial, especially in the farming communities; Jews must be made into "natural" men or women. The purpose of this noble ideal was to wean Jews from the occupation of middlemen in the European ghettos to primary producers in their own land. So, the characteristic refrain of that day among these Jewish pioneers was "We are coming to the land to build it and to be rebuilt by it." But this ideal, noble as it was, excluded Arabs from work on the newest, most ideological Jewish farms. This unfortunate result was created not by hatred of Arabs or by desire to do them harm. The motive of the Zionist pioneers was not wickedness, but what happened was a mixture of glory and tragedy.

After 1921 the tension between Jews and Arabs in Palestine seemed to be decreasing. Various explanations have been given for this change. The economy was improving, and so Arabs had less to make them angry. In the decade of the 1920s, Jewish immigration, especially from anti-Semitic Poland, was substantial, but Palestine was not being flooded by Jews, as the Arabs feared. The percentage of Jews in the population was small compared to the Arab majority: nearly one Jew to every five Arabs. But the chief reason for the few years of relative calm was probably the nature, then, of the government that Great Britain had established in the country. It was often accused, at the time and later, of being indifferent to the promises that had been made to the Jews, but the archives that are now open for research do not support this assertion. On the contrary, the Jews were benefiting from a government that remembered it had made a special promise to them, to help them build a national home of their own. Therefore, the British government used its power to suppress attacks on Jews, but this relative quiet did not last.

OPEN WARFARE ON AN EVER LARGER SCALE

Tension caused by age-old hatreds and nourished by religion ignited a major explosion between Jews and Arabs in 1929. The nub of the quarrel was over the right of Jews to freedom of worship at the Western Wall, the one part of the Temple in Jerusalem that still stood after all the rest had been destroyed in the year 70. For Arabs, the narrow alley between the Western Wall and some houses nearby was a thoroughfare for normal commerce. For Jews it was place for prayer. Inevitably, Jews tried to increase the sacred character of this alley, but Arabs kept driving donkeys through it to keep Jews from turning it into a kind of synagogue. The firebrands among the Arabs maintained that this was another example of the attempt by Jews to impose their needs and their tradition on Arabs, so the only effective response had to be the resort to violence. In riots in Jerusalem and the nearby city of Hebron dozens of Jews were murdered. The Jewish population in Hebron was forced out entirely. To be sure, there are accounts of Arab friends and neighbors saving the lives of Jews in Hebron by hiding them, but there are equally true accounts of neighbors and supposed friends joining those causing the outrage.

The possibility of cooperation between Arabs and Jews was severely damaged by the events of 1929. The lesson driven home for Jews was that Arabs could not be persuaded by reasonable arguments; they could be stopped only by force. The Palestinian Arabs were equally convinced that their cause could be upheld only by violence. Nonviolence meant, in the two decades between the wars and especially after 1929, three-cornered diplomacy involving Great Britain, the Jews, and the Arabs. No matter how favorably disposed the British government in London or its representatives who administered the mandate might seem to be to the Arab cause, they were not likely to nullify the basic commitment made in the Balfour Declaration that there be a Jewish national home in Palestine; the British could not, then, put the Jews of Palestine on boats and sail them to some distant shore that might or might not be willing to admit them. But the Arabs could imagine that keeping the situation heated and sporadically violent in Palestine would discourage further immigration and ultimately destroy the Zionist dream of creating a fully functioning society for Jews in Palestine.

In the 1930s this Arab hope became an embittered illusion. The cause was the rise of Adolf Hitler. In 1933, when he became the chancellor of Germany, he immediately began to enact a virulently anti-Semitic policy. At the same time, it was becoming more difficult for Jews on the run to find refuge in other European countries or elsewhere in the world. Palestine became a prime refuge precisely because, according to the mandate, the British had to admit Jews to the land. Arab resistance had succeeded to a considerable degree before 1933 in persuading some Jews to avoid immigration to Palestine and even in scaring some Jewish arrivals out of the country after they had been there for a while, but this was no longer true in the 1930s. The doors of the United States had been largely closed since 1924. In the years of dire need after 1933, when the Nazis ascended to power in Germany, Palestine was a key refuge. The Arabs might create obstacles and shoot at Jews, but many, some two hundred thousand between 1933 and 1940, had no choice but to come to Palestine.

This situation was, inevitably, a recipe for the escalation of already existing enmity. The Arabs in Palestine were becoming more warlike, because the Jewish population was now markedly increasing and the Jewish national home now seemed to have a large enough population, over four hundred thousand by the mid-1930s, to make it a viable and functioning entity. The Arabs therefore increased their violence against Jews, and Jews felt that they had no choice but to formalize their own organs of self-defense; they created a semiclandestine army in the semiclandestine Jewish state that was in the process of being formed.

By the mid-1930s the British knew that the situation was becoming untenable and that a solution to calm the hostilities had to be found. They created the highest level commission that was ever appointed under their auspices to survey the situation in Palestine and to propose some remedies. This was a royal commission chaired by Lord Peel. The members of this body were individuals who were widely regarded as impartial judges; they were not seen to be under the control of any British political faction. The Peel Commission took testimony from both Jewish and Arab leaders in both Palestine and London. In the spring of 1937 it announced its findings.

With sadness and regret, the commission could find no basis for peace between Jews and Arabs in Palestine. No set of arrangements could be imagined that would make it possible for them to live together in a single state:

> The application to Palestine of the Mandate System in general and of the specific Mandate in particular implied the belief that the obligations thus undertaken towards the Arabs and the Jews respectively would prove in course of time to be mutually com-

patible owing to the conciliatory effect on the Palestinian Arabs of the material prosperity which Jewish immigration would bring to Palestine as a whole. That belief has not been justified, and we see no hope of its being justified in future.

This intensification of the conflict will continue. The estranging force of conditions inside of Palestine is growing year by year. The educational systems, Arab and Jewish, are schools of nationalism, and they have only existed for a short time. The full effect on the rising generation has yet to be felt. And patriot "youth-movements," so familiar a feature of present-day politics in other countries of Europe or Asia, are afoot in Palestine. As each community grows, moreover, the rivalry between them deepens; the more numerous and prosperous the Arabs become, the more insistent will be their demand for their national independence and the more bitter their hatred of the obstacle that bars the way to it. As the Jewish National Home grows older and more firmly rooted, so will its self-confidence and political ambition.

Thus for internal and external reasons, it seems probable that the situation, bad as it now is, will grow worse. The conflict will go on, the gulf between Arabs and Jews will widen.

The Peel Commission therefore suggested that peace could best be served by the partition of the land into two states, one for the Jews and one for the Palestinian Arabs.

The city of Jerusalem, with some additions, should be administered separately by the British. In actual territory the Jews were being offered one-fifth of the land of Palestine and that fifth was not a continuous landmass. Within the borders of the proposed Jewish state, the Arab population would very nearly equal that of the Jews.

> These are the recommendations which we submit for dealing with the main grievances under the Mandate put before us by the Arabs and the Jews; but they are not, in our opinion, the recommendations which our terms of reference require. They will not, that is to say, "remove" the grievances nor "prevent their recurrence." They are the best palliatives we can devise for the disease from which Palestine is suffering, but they are only palliatives. They might reduce the inflammation and bring down the temperature, but they cannot cure the trouble. The disease is so deep-rooted that, in our firm conviction, the only hope of cure lies in a surgical operation.

Jews were dismayed by the borders that the Peel Commission proposed, but they were pleased that the suggestion of a Jewish state had now been put on the agenda of international politics. After a heated debate, the Zionist Congress held in the summer of 1937 accepted the suggestions made by the Peel Commission.

The Arabs rejected the findings of the Peel Commission in toto. For them it was not enough to have been awarded most of the land to be part of the Arab state of Jordan. Their fundamental objective was to make sure that a Jewish state not be allowed to arise. So, instead of being the signal for reduction of tension and a move toward peace for the two peoples, the Peel Commission report was the preamble for the most bitter fighting that had ever taken place in Palestine. By 1938 the Arabs in Palestine rebelled against Britain and also took to making war on Jews. Jews were fleeing before the increasingly murderous Nazis. The Arabs wanted to stop this immigration through violence. Essentially they succeeded.

The British government soon abandoned the proposals of the Peel Commission for compromise between Jews and Arabs. It decided it had to appease the Arabs. In their assessment of the situation as it existed in the late 1930s, the British could not keep putting more troops into Palestine to counter the revolt by the Arabs. The conflict in Palestine was eating up a sizable proportion of their military strength, and they had an empire to patrol and protect, one that then still covered nearly one-quarter of the globe. More immediately, Hitler's preparations for war were ever more unmistakable. In the late 1930s the British government had decided on a policy of appeasement. It was hoping to keep Nazi Germany from attacking in Europe.

The British government also decided that it was at least as prudent to appease the Arabs at the expense of the Jews. The result was that the British government handed the Arabs a clear-cut victory. It decided in 1939 to give the Jews a final grant of seventy-five thousand immigration spots for the next five years; thereafter there could be no more Jewish immigration into Palestine without Arab consent. The Jews were being told that whatever promise the British might have once made to them in the Balfour Declaration, the national home for the Jews would be peopled by a permanent Jewish minority, which would be subject, on the vital matter of immigration, to the will of the Arab majority.

As everyone expected, the Jews immediately and unequivocally rejected this White Paper. They could do no other. Jewish immigration into Palestine had grown substantially. Those who had hesitated to leave Germany had been hoping and even believing that Hitler was a passing phenomenon, but they knew by 1939 that he had become a threat to their lives. They were in flight from Germany and all of central Europe to find some country that would allow them to land. Most governments were not helpful. The Jewish people as a whole felt that only Palestine could not refuse homes to Jews in flight. They came legally, with valid certificates of immigration, and illegally, usually landing at night from small ships that had eluded the Royal Navy in the Mediterranean. The battle was joined between dire Jewish need and Arab resistance, but it was not merely a fight between Jews and Arabs. Since the British had now tilted toward the Arabs, they were no longer a neutral third party. Choking off immigration was now their own policy. Their major quarrel in Palestine had become their war with the Jews, who would not obey the orders of the British government.

This situation was not alleviated by the outbreak of World War II in the beginning of September 1939. Even though Jews were in clear danger as the Nazis swept westward through all of Europe and conquered all of the continent north of the Pyrenees and the Alps, the White Paper was not abrogated. Jews could not come to Palestine in any substantial number and no major effort of any kind was made to bring them to their national home.

The Arabs of Palestine were essentially indifferent to the travails of the British in World War II. No attempt was made to provide Arab volunteers for the British army, even in 1942, when the German North Africa corps under General Rommel was approaching Egypt and threatening to march on to Palestine. On the contrary, the most notable spokesman and leader of the Arabs in Palestine, the Grand Mufti of Jerusalem, Haj Amin al-Husseini, had left Palestine and joined Hitler. He expected as his reward for this alliance that the Nazis would uproot or destroy the Jews in Palestine and thus solve the Palestinian Arabs' "Jewish problem."

The Jews of Palestine chose a radically different path. Immediately after the outbreak of war, they volunteered in large numbers (some twenty thousand) and began to agitate for the creation of a distinctive Jewish force within the British army. This body was to be made up of volunteers from Jewish Palestine. There was considerable opposition to this proposal within elements of the British government, for fear that a Jewish military force would upset the Arabs and that it would not be completely obedient to its British commanders. These Jews were suspected of objectives of their own, such as saving endangered Jews in Europe or remaining organized to fight at the end of the war for Zionist aims in Palestine. Despite the wrangling, the Jewish Brigade was finally formed in 1944. It was to do important work in Europe in helping the survivors of the Holocaust and illegal immigrants into Palestine in the years between the end of the war in 1945 and the Israel's declaration of independence in 1948.

THE HOLOCAUST AND ITS CONSEQUENCES

The decade of the 1940s was the profound turning point of Jewish history in the last century. For the Zionists in Israel and for those who admired them all over the world, the 1940s was the occasion for several radical reassessments of the place of Jews in the world. At the end of World War II, it was immediately apparent that the remaining Jews of central and eastern Europe, those who were still alive after the Nazis and their helpers had murdered six million of their brethren, had no homes to which they could return. The Germans and their collaborators in every country the German army had conquered during the war had taken over Jewish homes, businesses, and property. They had destroyed the synagogues and the bulk of Jewish communal buildings. The books in the libraries and the artifacts in the museums had been confiscated. Whatever was found had to be traced to the places to which they had been "deported." Most important of all, Europe was poisoned with anti-Semitism. The dominant outcry almost everywhere expressed the desire to keep the Jews from coming back. The few that did find their way back to their former homes were often in mortal danger. In 1946 in Kielce, Poland, there was a bloody pogrom in which over sixty Jews were killed in order to terrify those who might want to follow after them and return home, and individuals and small groups of returning Jews were murdered in many other places.

The alternative was clear: the Jewish refugees had to get out of Europe. In actual fact, a number of the survivors did find haven in western Europe and some were admitted to the United States, but a hard core of at least a hundred thousand survivors remained in camps for Displaced Persons (DP), which were located for the most part in the American zone of occupation in Germany. An overwhelming consensus soon arose in all quarters of the international Jewish community that this hundred thousand must be allowed to immigrate to Palestine. The British government balked at this. It maintained that it was still bound by its White Paper of 1938, which had ruled that Jewish immigration into Palestine should be ended except in the unlikely event that the Arabs agreed otherwise.

The Jewish answer to this British obstruction was illegal immigration. For the two years immediately after the end of the war, from 1945 to 1947, ships were chartered in southern European ports and substantial convoys of refugees were brought by devious routes from the DP camps to board these boats. These leaky tubs went out into the Mediterranean, those aboard knowing that almost all the boats would be found by the Royal Navy and kept from discharging their passengers on the shores of Palestine. The British established holding camps for these refugees in Cyprus, but those who dared sail on the boats felt that it would be better to be held in Cyprus than to languish in the camps in Germany.

The fierce battles over the immigration of the survivors of Nazism kept the question of the future of the Jews after the war in the foreground of world concern. Indeed, the British general who commanded the sector of British occupation in Germany complained bitterly in those days that there were many refugees of all kinds in central Europe as a result of the war, but the Jews kept insisting on "rushing to the head of the queue."[4] But no matter how great the suffering of those of all the other nationalities, none but the Jews had been singled out by the Nazis for total destruction. None but the Jews had lost the vast majority of their kind who lived in Europe. None but the Jews had come out of the war fearing that, because the destruction had been so intense, they might be on the way to becoming extinct as a people. So the Jews fought back. Their demand for large-scale, immediate entry into Palestine, into the place where they had been promised a national home, was not negotiable.

On the other side, the Arabs were at least as intransigent. They had no doubt that, if the doors of Palestine were indeed opened to all the Jews who were then in need of refuge, the local Arab population of Palestine would be transformed into a minority. Never mind that some of the Jewish leaders kept insisting that the lives of the Arabs would, in fact, be made better by large-scale Jewish immigration and the increased economic activity it would generate. This argument was blunted by increased Arab resentment at being outmaneuvered and soon outgunned in a country they regarded as their own and as part of the Islamic world. From the Arab point of view, only one tactic would lead to victory: violence and war. This was not violence intended to secure better conditions or a larger share of power for Arabs in a land that contained two nationalities. It was an avowed and uncompromising attack on the growing Jewish presence in the land. The objective was to drive the Jews out, so the years from 1945 to 1947 were years of intense guerrilla warfare in Palestine.

The "Jewish problem" had now become an explosive international question that world opinion could not ignore. The newly formed United Nations (UN) had to find some acceptable solution for the future of the survivors in Europe of the Nazi attempt to exterminate all of the Jews within their reach. Clearly, world powers had not saved the Jews from the Nazis, as their predecessors had not, for many centuries, protected the Jews from attacks by pogrom makers, Crusaders, and other enemies. However, world leaders had to take account of the fact that the Arabs were unalterably opposed to an increase in the Jewish presence in Palestine and even more to any notion that the two peoples could live together in one political state when it seemed clear to the Arabs that they would soon be dominated by the dynamism of the Jews.

Great Britain and the United States studied the question through the special Anglo-American Commission in 1946, which came back with a majority report that echoed the findings of the Peel Commission a decade earlier in 1937: the Jews and the Arabs of Palestine were not in the country because they desired to establish a binational state and to live together in peace, but each had an undeniable, though differently motivated, claim on all of the land. The next year, the UN study suggested that the closest approximation to a viable solution (no claim was made that either side would be granted what it would regard as absolute justice) was the partition of the land into two states, one Jewish and the other Palestinian. This solution granted the Jews a bit more than half of the 12,000 square miles that compose the territory of Palestine west of the Jordan River.

After this report events moved rapidly. On November 29, 1947, the General Assembly of the UN, meeting at Lake Success, New York, voted by the necessary margin of more than two to one to approve the partition plan. The Jews were not happy with the small territory they had been awarded, but they accepted the partition resolution and agreed to set up their state in the land allotted to them. The Arab Higher Committee denounced the plan and went to war against it. This meant that by May 14, 1948, when the plan was to go into effect, a Jewish state was indeed proclaimed in Tel Aviv, but the Arabs made no move toward accepting any transfer of power to the Jews in their supposed area. The closest thing to acceptance of the plan by any Arab power was, as we now know, the quiet understanding between the Jewish authorities and Emir Abdullah of Transjordan that his troops would enter the Arab areas of what became the West Bank and that he would de facto assume control of the region. That did not stop Abdullah from playing a role in the war that almost all of the surrounding Arab states declared on the nascent state of Israel.

THE WAR OF 1948–49 FOR JEWS AND ARABS: TWO CONTRASTING NARRATIVES

On the morning of May 14 in 1948 the British authorities took down their flag and the High Commissioner sailed away aboard a British ship from Haifa Harbor. That afternoon a solemn assembly in Tel Aviv heard David Ben-Gurion read Israel's Declaration of Independence and announce the creation of the state of Israel. Arab armies from the states that surrounded Israel (except Lebanon) were on the move into the territory that had been allotted by the United Nations and the armed Arabs everywhere in Palestine were in a shooting war with Jews. The hostilities were stopped several times by truces ordered by the United Nations and they finally came to an end in January 1949. Israel had established itself by the force of its own arms and the Arabs had lost the war.

The war's most striking result was to increase Jewish-held territory from 6,200 square miles, as envisaged in the UN partition plan, to 8,000—that is, the Jews conquered all of the Negev and more territory in the north of the country. Two narratives of this war arose almost immediately. For the Jews it was and has remained the "War of Independence." For Arabs it was and has remained *an-Nakba* ("the Catastrophe"). The Arabs have usually taken great pains not to ascribe the fault for this disaster to themselves, even though there has been a large amount of recrimination over the inadequate support of the Palestinian cause by the Arab states. One seldom finds any mention in the discussion by the Arabs or their partisans that the war that they lost in 1948–49 was an attack on a UN resolution. The Arabs, with almost no exceptions, agreed that they had the right to defy the UN because any settlement that did not give the Palestinian Arabs total victory over the Jews was an intolerable affront.

This entrenched unwillingness to compromise has also colored, from that day forward, the question of the

Palestinian refugees who fled their homes during the war. It has become a subject of major argument among historians and political pamphleteers (they are often the same) as to whether the seven hundred thousand Palestinian Arabs who left their homes were pushed out deliberately by the Jews or whether they left on the presumption that they would be coming back very soon with the triumphant Arab armies. The first of the contemporary historians to tackle this question, Benny Morris, has concluded that a majority of the Palestinian refugees left to get out of the way of the hostilities, and some or many of them did indeed hope to come back home soon as part of the Arab victory over the Jews; a minority were pushed out by Israeli forces. The question is nonetheless moot.

I myself was in Israel in 1949 as the war was winding down, and I got to know a number of the Israeli commanders. I asked every one of these new friends whether they had ever been given any orders to expel Palestinians. The only such action to which one of the officers admitted was the order to remove, on very short notice, some fifty thousand Arabs from the towns of Lydda (now Lod) and Ramleh. These hostile Arab towns sat astride and cut off the main road between Tel Aviv and Jerusalem. On the other hand, not a single one of the military commanders with whom I spoke in 1949 seemed to have regarded it as one of his prime tasks to persuade the Arabs not to flee.

The story that Israeli trucks carrying loudspeakers had gone through the Arab neighborhood of Haifa assuring Arabs that they had nothing to fear was indeed being repeated (in fact, there were just a few posters to that effect), but the reason for that effort was soon forgotten. Arabs played an important role in running the oil depots in Haifa; without them these installations would have been difficult to maintain. Therefore, it was in their Jewish co-workers' interest to persuade these Arabs to remain. But there was no such reason to persuade the bulk of the Arabs on the run to remain within the boundaries of the part of Palestine that Israel had been given by the partition resolution or the part they were conquering in the war of 1948–49.

In my own quest for the facts in the summer of 1949, I did get one revealing response. One of the commanders (who became and remained a friend to the end of his days) did tell me that he went to see the supreme commander, David Ben-Gurion, to ask him about the Arabs who had run away and who were beginning to show some signs of wanting to come back. At the beginning of the war there had been some four hundred thousand Arabs in the territory that was to become Jewish; by the end of hostilities, their number had decreased to about one hundred thousand. Ben-Gurion replied to the question not by giving a direct order, either to bring these refugees back to their homes or to keep them out. He answered with a question: "And what would you have me do with all these Arabs?" Ben-Gurion did not order that the Arabs be chased out, but he clearly had no desire to be confronted by a Jewish state in which Jewish and Arab populations were nearly equal in number.

During the end of the war of 1948–49 the United Nations stepped in several times to force cease-fires. Eventually both Jews and Arabs agreed to an armistice. Under UN auspices there was a round of conferences between Israel and each one of the Arab states that had gone to war against it. The result of these meetings was a set of supposedly temporary arrangements that it was expected would soon lead to formal peace treaties. This did not happen. There were some contacts between Israel and Jordan, and Israel and Syria, which seemed to be a first step toward peace, but these very preliminary efforts failed completely. Supposedly, the Arabs did not make peace with Israel because they, as the losers in the war of 1948–49, were too weak. More probably, the Arabs did not make peace with Israel then because they had not sorted out for themselves whether they had to make peace at all. They had not accepted the notion that Israel might be in the Middle East to stay. They had gone to war to make its existence impossible, and they could not reverse themselves simply because they had lost the war.

On the Jewish side, most felt that they had "bought" the right to the buildings and farms that the Arabs had abandoned by their victory in war and by their sacrifice; some six thousand of a total population of six hundred thousand had fallen in this bloodiest of all of Israel's wars. Within the next several years this feeling of entitlement was rooted, as well, in events that were happening in the Arab world. Ancient Jewish communities that had been left in Arab countries from Yemen and Iraq through Egypt, Algeria, Tunis, Morocco, and in Iran, felt that they were endangered by the new tension between Jews and the Arab world as a whole. Most of these Jews fled to Israel, leaving homes and properties. Opinion in Israel held that the Arab world had taken at least as much from the Jews as Israeli Jews had taken from the Palestinian Arabs. There had been an exchange of people and of property. As in many aspects of the Israeli-Palestinian or Jewish-Arab confrontation, here too, on the matter of the result of fleeing from the scene of war, the combatants were talking past each other out of different scripts.[5]

As a result of the war of 1948–49 each side had a new and more potent reason for increased hostility toward the other. The Jews now knew beyond any shadow of a doubt that the Arabs remained entrenched in opposition to the results of the Balfour Declaration. They were reaffirming their well-established principle that the Jews must be humbled and, if possible, expelled. The Jews, for their part, knew that Arab enmity toward them had grown. Despite decades of earlier rhetoric by Jewish liberals about peaceful coexistence between the two warring nationalities, by the end of the war of 1948–49 Israelis had largely concluded that the Arabs would be kept in check only by superior power. Soon the Palestinians began a policy of infiltrating across the cease-fire lines to make Israel insecure and frightened. The seeds of distrust in the notion of an independent Palestinian state were being sown among the Jews. The suggestion of an independent Palestinian state had been the main proposal of the UN Commission in 1947. If a state in Palestinian hands meant granting Arabs the power to infiltrate across the armistice lines, Israel might still pay some homage to the idea of a two-state solution, but it was no longer willing to contemplate an Arab Palestinian entity that it did not essentially control militarily.

Soon after the end of the Six-Day War in June 1967, the Israelis knew they had to think about what was to be done with the West Bank. The dominant idea at the time was proposed by Yigal Allon, who had been one of the highest commanders during Israel's War of Independence; he was generally regarded as a future prime minister (he never arrived at that distinction before his relatively early death). Allon proposed that Israel remain in control of the Jordan Valley by putting down quasi-military settlements as buffers against infiltration and that the Israeli army permanently occupy the hills to its west. In Allon's view this was the minimum that would be required to make sure that the Palestinians would not be in a position to mount a serious attack against Israel. Some hope still remained in Israel that the question of Palestinian refugees could be solved by letting some back into their homes ("to reunite families") and by resettlement of all the rest, with substantial Israeli and international help. Israel wanted to view the Arab refugee question as a humanitarian concern and not as a continuing political problem—that is, Israel was willing to calculate what it might have to do to help make an end of the sense of displacement felt by these seven hundred thousand refugees and their descendants, but it did not recognize it as a national question.

In actual fact, something very deep was changing in the theories on which the Israeli-Arab relationship was based. The Jews had assumed for centuries, long before the beginning of the modern Zionist endeavor, that the Arabs in Palestine were part of a larger entity, the Arab, overwhelmingly Muslim, people in the Middle East. Indeed, this was then the view of the Arabs themselves. In 1938 a leading Arab intellectual, George Antonius (who happened to be a Lebanese Christian), published a work describing and en-

couraging what he called the "Arab awakening."[6] His ire was
directed against Great Britain and France, the dominant
Western powers in the region, and against the Jewish Zionists who had established their beachhead in the Arab world.
In Antonius's view these beachheads were expressions of
colonialism, on the presumption so prevalent in the West
that Europeans could freely control the Muslim world and
determine its future to suit themselves. Antonius was writing about the time the Peel Commission was in session, and
he knew that the Jewish representatives, including such di-
verse figures as Chaim Weizmann, the leader of mainstream
Zionists, and Vladimir Jabotinsky, the head of a group of
much more radical nationalists called revisionist Zionists,
regarded the quarrel over the Zionist endeavors as a battle
between the Jewish and Arab worlds. This definition of the
angry encounter made it possible for the Jews to think into
the 1950s and some years beyond that the Arabs of Palestine
really belonged to a larger entity, the Arab world. Culturally
and emotionally it should be relatively easy for them to find
new homes in the region. This seemed all the more possible,
even probable, because some of the Arabs in Palestine had
come rather recently, since the Zionist effort had begun,
from neighboring lands because economic opportunities for
Arabs had been increased by the activity that the Jews had
brought to the new Palestine.

Much has been made since by some Jewish debaters who
have argued that this Arab immigration into Palestine had
been substantial, so that a near majority of the Arabs in Palestine had been there for only two generations or so. There is an
obvious counter to this polemical point: the overwhelming

bulk of Jewish population in the land had been there for less than two generations as well. The truth is that the amount of Arab immigration into Palestine was at most 15 percent of the total Arab population.[7] Regardless of the numbers involved, in the minds of Jews and Arabs alike the quarrel had not been defined as a Jewish-Palestinian conflict. On the contrary, in those years the literature of Arab anger at defeat and dispossession in the war for Palestine was full of denunciation of the Arab powers that had not done enough for their Palestinian brethren, who were flesh of their flesh, blood of their blood, and no less Arab and Muslim than the inhabitants of the states surrounding the land on which an-Nakba had taken place.

But the situation was changing. It has been said, repeatedly and conventionally, that the Palestinians were created as a separate identity by their unique experience of having to cope with Zionism in Palestine and that, indeed, Palestinian nationalism exists as a shadow of Zionism. From rethinking the history of the conflict and rereading large numbers of Arab statements and documents from the 1950s and 1960s, it has become clear that the seal was set on the sense of the Palestinians as a separate entity by the way the Arabs in the surrounding lands treated the refugees from Palestine. It was not just that the Zionists had either indirectly or directly pushed them out; it was equally painful that their Arab brethren would not take them in. In all the neighboring Arab states they were kept in refugee camps or left to their own devices or to the mercies of alms from the UN. Only Jordan granted them citizenship.

Arthur Hertzberg

THE PALESTINIANS REDEFINE PALESTINE
AS A SMALL, ORIGINAL NATION

Here was the beginning of a new major rift between the way in which Israelis and Palestinians thought of the conflict. It continued to be convenient for the Israelis to regard themselves as being confronted by the whole of the Arab world. Never mind that Israel had won a convincing victory in 1948–49 against the armies of all Arabs in the region. The fact remained that Arab population in the Middle East was at least sixty times the size of Jewish Israel's. The menacing rhetoric that came from the Arab world and the Palestinians themselves was experienced as a large and continuing threat. Even after winning the war for its independence, Israel retained the mind-set inherited from the cultural experience of being Jewish in a non-Jewish world; it thought of itself as a new, "normal," state, but it could not completely shake the victim mentality.

On the other hand, even after their defeat in war, the Arabs could not lay claim to that painful but sometimes useful label. How could they play the eternal victim if they were flexing their muscles, at least verbally, for the vengeance that they would soon wreak upon Israel. But the Palestinians had lost the war and the bulk of them were friendless refugees. If they could define themselves as a separate nationality, a distinct group among the Arabs of the Middle East, as the Egyptians, for example, were distinct from the Syrians or the Saudis, then the conflict would become a battle between Israeli Jews and Palestinian Arabs. These two groups were comparable in size, but with one distinction. The Israelis were becoming more powerful and making a success of their endeavors; the Palestinians were miserable and seemed to have little hope of returning to their homes or even gaining some political base. But defining Palestinian identity as different from, and even unlike, any other Arab identity could make the claim of being the victim believable.

This question of self-definition has been renegotiated in recent years by two Palestinian intellectuals who live and work in America. Rashid Khalidi, in his book *Palestinian Identity,* suggests that some Palestinians began to have a sense of their separate identity in the twelfth century, when they encountered the Crusaders as they established their kingdom in Jerusalem. Khalidi qualifies this assertion by maintaining that "several overlapping senses of identity are involved in the process of how Palestinians have come to define themselves as a people." Khalidi argues that "identity for the Palestinians is and has always been intermingled with a sense of identity on so many other levels, whether Islamic or Christian, Ottoman or Arab, local or universal, or family and tribal." So, at the dawn of conflict between Zionists and the Palestinian Arabs late in the nineteenth century, the Palestinians "had multiple loyalties to their religion, the Ottoman state, the Arabic language, and the emerging identity of Arabism, as well as their country and local and familial foci." This subtle and nuanced description allows Khalidi to have it both ways: there is a very old element of Palestinian self-awareness, but it exists in association with other forces, especially the sense of belonging to the Arab nation as a whole. The arrival of the Zionists forced the Palestinians to define themselves more sharply and more separately from all the rest of the Arabs, who did not have to fight directly with the Jews for the possession of the same land—but Palestinian consciousness could, even so, be a complicated mixture of larger Arab loyalties and more immediate commitments to place or family or tribe.[8]

Rashid Khalidi is a scholar of consequence who describes very carefully a Palestinian identity caught between the pulls of various loyalties. In his view the Palestinians became one after their defeat in the war of 1948–49 and the exile of some seven hundred thousand from their homes. "If the Arab population of Palestine had not been sure of their identity before 1948, the experience of defeat, dispossession, and exile guaranteed that they knew what their identity was very soon afterwards: they were Palestinians. The refugee experience, the callous treatment by Israel and several of the Arab host states, and the shared trauma of 1948, which all still had to come to terms with, cemented and universalized a common identity as Palestinians."

The merit of Khalidi's account as scholarship is that it has almost no overt polemics. He is free enough to talk of Israel as a fact and to describe it, at least in Israel's own view, as a great historic achievement of substantial moral significance. In his concluding pages, Khalidi accepts as a matter of course that the Israeli state and society will continue to exist. And yet the subtext of his book is clear: the Zionists built Israel on the destruction of the Palestinian nation. They did not acquire some backwater of the larger Arab world. On the contrary, they brought their own state into being by trying to make an end of a people with a history of its own, the Palestinians. Khalidi insists that the probable and seemingly inevitable solution of finally enacting partition must take account of the deep injury to the Palestinians, who have so far been denied their own self-determination and sacrificed to Zionist aims.

A more vehement proponent of Khalidi's thesis is Muhammad Muslih. I have not been able to find in any of his writings even one mention of the state of Israel. He seems to will its nonexistence by speaking only of the battle between Arab nationalism, or alternatively Palestinian nationalism, and the Zionists. Muslih takes great pains to insist that Palestinian nationalism has a history of its own. It was developing its own nature quite apart from the encounter of the Palestinians with the Zionists in the past century. In the concluding pages of his book, *The Origins of Palestinian Nationalism*, Muslih makes much of a session of the Palestinian Arab Congress that took place in December 1920. He tries to establish the Palestinian nature of the meeting by mentioning a discussion of a local concern, the excessive price of crops. But, as Muslih himself tells us, the major resolution of that meeting was a unanimous request of Great Britain

> to establish a "national government responsible to a representative assembly, whose members would be chosen from the Arabic-speaking people who have been inhabiting Palestine until the outbreak of the War." By so doing Britain will be honoring, according to the resolution, the "noble principles which it seeks to apply in Arabic-speaking Iraq and Transjordan, and will be enhancing and consolidating the

deep-rooted friendship existing between Britain and the entire Arab nation."

Having quoted a resolution that appeals to Britain in the name of the "entire Arab nation," Muslih concludes by insisting that "the idea of unity with Syria, or even the idea of pan-Arab unity, was completely forsaken." Continuing to try to have it both ways, Muslih writes near the end of his book,

> We may conclude, therefore, that Zionism did not create Palestinian nationalism. What Zionism did was provide the Palestinians with a focus for their national struggle. In other words, Zionism was the focus of the Palestinians and the pivot around which their politics centered.[9]

It is particularly revealing that three years after Muslih published his magnum opus, *The Origins of Palestinian Nationalism*, to make the case that origins of Palestinian nationalism had nothing to do with Zionism, he published an essay, "The Rise of Local Nationalism in the Arab East," in a collection in which he ascribes the rise of Palestinian nationalism to the Syrian Arab nationalists who were "relegating" the Palestinian cause to a secondary post. Muslih goes on to say,

> Zionism and the imposition of the Mandate system provided the spark and added to the fuel that had

already been there. Early in 1920 a perceptive Zionist agent offered an astute summation of the consequences of the clash of political priorities in the Syrian arena. He described the fracturing of the Arab nationalist movement and predicted the emergence of what he called the "Arab Nationalist Movement of Palestine."[10]

So what does all this mean? This account of the "origins of Palestinian nationalism" is not history, but a contemporary political pamphlet. The Palestinian cause needs for internal purposes, in order to maintain sympathy or at the very least guilt in the Arab world, to situate the Palestinians as part of the larger *umma,* or Arab people. On the other hand, the Zionists cannot be allowed to imagine that their quarrel is with the whole of the *umma* and that, therefore, the Arab world as a whole should find it possible to make peace with the loss of sovereignty over a few thousand square miles of land for Israel on the periphery of its large expanse. It remains necessary, of course, for his argument that Muslih deny what is visibly so, that the particular situation of the Palestinians is a creation of the growth of the Zionist presence and of the battle against it. Obviously, a proponent of Palestinian nationalism cannot bring himself to give the Zionists such credit. That would "anoint" the Zionists as the causative factor in the creation of the passion and the separate political identity of the Palestinians.

In the new situation of the early years of the state of Israel and the Palestinian refugee problem, Jews and Arabs had returned to their by now classic and repetitive themes. Arabs were finding new ways of being angry with those who had not done for them what they always failed to do for themselves—push the Jews out. But the meaning of the Zionist venture was that the Jews were coming to Palestine in desperation because they had nowhere else to go: they were coming to be in control of their own destiny. With all the sympathy and understanding that did exist in the Jewish world for the pain of the Arabs, the Jews could not simply rush to the boats and get out.

On the contrary, in the 1950s, quite apart from the hundreds of thousands who were coming to the new state of Israel from the DP camps in Europe, at least half a million came from Yemen, North Africa, Egypt, and Iraq. They did not feel safe in the lands of their birth because the atmosphere between Arabs and Jews had become so poisonous. It has even been argued in recent years by Jewish debaters that the Jewish exodus from Arab lands, a number roughly equal to that of Palestinian Arabs who fled from Zionist Israel, was a de facto exchange of populations. So, on both sides polemical points abound, almost without number. But one question must remain constant and always before us: Can we really believe that in the past one hundred years many Jews on the run had any alternative but to come in large numbers to Palestine to save their lives and to create their own national home and political and cultural identity?

From the very beginning of the Zionist endeavor, one unalterable and nonnegotiable principle was at the center of the effort to achieve for Jews the unlimited right of immigration into the homeland. When the state of Israel was proclaimed in 1948, the right of return was ordained in its Declaration of Independence as the right that could be claimed by any Jew in the world. Obviously, more will need to be said about this fundamental characteristic of Zionism and of the state of Israel, which it created, especially in the light of the attacks in the name of the democratic principle of "one man, one vote" that have been leveled against this self-definition of Israel. I am deferring this ever more pointed and emotional contemporary discussion to Chapter 3, but one point needs to be made here.

The battle for unlimited immigration and the enactment of the law of return as Israel's first act as a sovereign state reflected the great fear of Jews in the twentieth century: the mass of Jews might again have to be on the move. The Zionist movement refuses to surrender the commitment to keep ports and airfields open under the control of essentially Jewish Israel.

On the other side, among the Palestinian Arabs, it is equally true that there is one unbending principle still shared not only by most Palestinians but by the overwhelming majority of the Arab world: the Jewish presence in Palestine, and especially the creation of an independent Jewish state, is an act of aggression. War against Israel is legitimate because Palestine, with its Arab majority, did not belong to the Western powers, which had no right to give any part of this land away to solve their problems with the Jews. Therefore, with only a handful of exceptions, the Arabs of Palestine have never budged from their conviction that the Zionist state is an alien body; it does not belong in their region and certainly not in the land the Palestinians claim for themselves. The refugees from the Catastrophe of the Arab defeat in 1948–49 and their descendants, numbering more than three million, claim a right to return to the land from which they are now excluded.

To be sure, there has been an increasing amount of discussion in recent years about some forms of compromise, so that the Palestinian refugees might return in token numbers to Israel, be free to settle in the West Bank when it becomes a Palestinian state, or be given compensation to enable them to move and settle down outside the region, but these discussions have never seized the imagination of a Palestinian majority. By far the dominant position remains what it has been for more than a century since the Zionists came to settle in Palestine: let us refuse to find ways of compromising with the existence of the Zionist entity; let us make uncompromising war.

Is there a way out? We can face this question only if we examine more precisely the root and sources of Palestinian Arab anger.

THREE

◇◇◇◇◇◇◇◇◇

ARABS FIGHT JEWS

T he deadly clash has never gone away. Indeed, it has become more embittered, especially since the 1930s, when the issue of what to do with Palestine moved to the center of international political concern. The Israelis and the Palestinians have become deeply involved as antagonists in all of the contemporary political issues. In World War II the Jews were on the side of the Western alliance and the Palestinians were either neutral or, through the Grand Mufti of Jerusalem, in the Nazi camp. The Arab world as a whole was opposed to colonialism, and it remained vehemently angry at the Zionist Jews who had established a supposedly colonialist presence in the Middle East. Few Arabs understood that many of the Jews who came to Palestine and later to Israel in the twentieth century were fleeing for their lives, and most of the time they had little choice to go anywhere other than to Palestine or Israel. Throughout most of the twentieth century Jews coming to Palestine and Arabs resident in the country competed for the "honor" of being the principal victim of life in general and the struggle between them in particular. The result of their battle is a paradox: in confrontation with the Palestinians, the Israelis are very much more powerful, but the Arab world as a whole, even with its sharp divisions, remains an ever larger threat for the future of Israel.

The first Arab protest against the new Jewish arrivals in Palestine was made in a telegram from Jerusalem in 1891 that asked the Grand Vizier of the Ottoman Empire to prohibit Russian Jews from coming to Palestine and buying land.[1] This telegram was sent by Muslims, even though some Muslim notables refused to sign it. The authors of this protest defined two fundamental requests, which remained for the next half century the basic Arab position: the end of Jewish immigration and the end of Jewish acquisition of land. By 1904 the battle had been defined in overt, stark terms by a Maronite Christian writer, Négib Azoury, who had studied in France and come under the influence of the French anti-Semites who were arrayed against Captain Alfred Dreyfus, the Jewish officer in the general staff who had been wrongly convicted in 1894 of treason against France. Azoury's book, *Le Réveil de la Nation Arabe* ("The Awakening of the Arab Nation"), contains a very dark forecast for the future of Arab-Jewish relations:

> Two important phenomena, of the same nature but opposed, which have still not drawn anyone's attention, are emerging at this moment in Asiatic Turkey. They are the awakening of the Arab nation and the latent effort of the Jews to reconstitute on a very large scale the ancient kingdom of Israel. Both these movements are destined to fight each other

continually until one of them wins. The fate of the entire world will depend on the final result of this struggle between these two peoples representing two contrary principles.[2]

There have been variations in this story through the years. While the British held the mandate for Palestine, attempts at compromise suggested that the Jews could continue to come to Palestine only in the numbers the land could support through its "absorptive capacity," but this formula never stopped the quarrel or the violence. Who was to judge what the absorptive capacity of the land really was? An industrialized society can absorb far more people than a state of peasants, but it is precisely a modern economy (because the Jews are much more experienced in managing such an enterprise than the Arabs) that the Arabs wanted to slow down in Palestine. In desperation, several times it was suggested that Jews could come to Palestine, even in moments of dire need such as the 1930s after Hitler came to power in Germany, only in numbers agreed upon by Arab leaders on behalf of their people; but no such agreement was ever forthcoming. The number to which Arabs would agree was always the same: zero. This was still the PLO position in the 1970s and 1980s, when immigration had been under the control of a functioning Jewish state for decades after 1948.

In the acrimonious battle for the right to come to Palestine, many Jews kept invoking the claim rooted not in their religion ("God gave us the land"), but in history: Jews had defined their national identity in this land some three thousand years ago, and they had never forgotten their attachment to it; life outside the land was always defined as *galut,* "exile." Arabs countered that Jews had not dwelt in the land in any numbers since a long, long time ago. In more recent centuries, and certainly since the birth of Islam in the seventh century, the overwhelming number of the inhabitants of Palestine were Arabs. Nowhere else in the world have the descendants of a tribe that last dwelt in a land thousands of years ago returned and claimed possession. But the Jews kept insisting that their rights were superior to those of the existing majority.

Inevitably, this argument moved in two directions. The Jews made much of their historic connection to the land. Indeed, the most widespread fad among Jews in the land, both before and after the state of Israel was declared, was to search in archeological digs for evidence of Jewish presence and creativity in past times. Jews may have been few in the land for many centuries, but they were never quite absent, and those who were there maintained the continuity of the tie of the entire Jewish people, scattered as it was in all its diasporas, to the land of Israel. This argument was never convincing to the overwhelming majority of Arabs. Almost without exception they claimed that all of the shrines of Jewish religion and history belong not to the Jews, but to Muslims. The Tomb of the Ancestors, of the Patriarchs and the Matriarchs, in Hebron was a Muslim shrine and Jews were not permitted to enter this mosque. Jews were barely tolerated at the place holiest of all for them, the Western Wall, which still stood as the only remnant of the Second Temple. Almost no one ever heeded the plea that the angry combatants should compromise on mutual respect for each other's history.

The Jews had to fall back on the basic argument that their place in Palestine was far more important to them, and to the world, than denying them that place could possibly mean to the Arabs. But here lurked a problem, a very deep problem, which is nowhere near solution. The Jewish case was based on the proposition that the party of the second part, the opponent, was the whole Arab world. No one had ever described the half million inhabitants in Palestine in the nineteenth and early twentieth centuries as anything more than a modest and undistinguished part of Arab society as a whole. Its cultural centers, past and present, were elsewhere, in Egypt, Syria, and Iraq. The vast expanse of the Arab world could afford to look away as the Jews were coming to Palestine (so the Jews argued), because the lack of sovereignty in that land would not vitally affect the culture and the self-respect of the mass of the Arabs.

As long as the conflict could be defined in these broad terms, Zionists essentially had little trouble in being of good conscience. Never mind that in the 1940s some Arab spokesmen changed the terms of the debate by insisting that Jews should demand as their recompense for all the horrors the West had visited upon them a territory of their own in a piece of Germany or perhaps of Poland. Why should Muslims in the Arab world "pay"? They (so the Arab narrative went) had always treated Jews better than Christians and other Westerners had.

But after the Holocaust, most of the survivors wanted to go home, to the land in which their people had defined themselves more than twenty centuries before. As we have seen in the previous chapter, the most sophisticated spokesmen for the Palestinian cause have recently "discovered," in the 1990s, that a Palestinian national consciousness quite different from that of the rest of the Arabs had long existed. The battle against "Zionist aggression" was now defined as the desperate attempt to preserve this local identity. Thus the issue could be described as a bitter quarrel between two nationalisms, Israeli and Palestinian: two peoples have been and are fighting over one and the same land. Public sympathy can thus shift to the Palestinians as the new victims and the Israelis can be accused of behaving like conquerors.

But the argument for the existence of a separate Palestinian identity for many centuries is flimsy. What has not been proven is that this supposed Palestinian tradition produced elements of any importance to Arab Islamic culture. The Palestinians really entered history after the Zionists arrived. They learned from them how to conduct a modern national movement and they defined themselves by opposing their Zionist teachers. The Palestinians became a separate Arab tribe—they entered contemporary history—as they tried to stem the flood of Zionism. They went to battle to keep Palestine for themselves, which meant, in their minds, that they would be keeping Palestine for the Arab world as a whole.

But the Jews are still fearful. They may appear today to be powerful in Israel, and to be an important element in the life of the United States, but as a people the Jews have not been able to slough off the many centuries of underlying discomfort and worry about their future. In many places in the world Jewish life continues to be uncertain and insecure, and Zionist Israel is now under fierce attack. Its enemies often talk the language not of national conflict, but of anti-Semitism and the desire to destroy Israel and humble the Jews. Today, Jews are less likely than in more confident days to surrender their right under the law of return for those in need to find refuge in Israel.

A CENTURY OF ARAB OPPOSITION TO ZIONISM

But when did Arab anger really start? Was it really full-blown at the very beginning of the new Jewish presence in Palestine in the last decades of the nineteenth century?

One ought not be too dogmatic, to claim that there was always nothing but emnity. At the very beginning there were occasions when Jews were greeted with guns, but there is also some evidence that friendly relations did exist between new Jewish farmers and Arabs in the vicinity. This amicability even extended into business relations in the cities. Those who tell of this experience of goodwill generally ascribe it to the economic advances these new Jewish immigrants were bringing to some Arabs. On the farms in those days Jews were employing ten Arabs for every Jewish worker employed. The Jews in the cities began as clients of the Arab shopkeepers who were already in business.

The most important reason for the goodwill of those days was, however, Arab certainty that Jews were coming in relatively negligible numbers and were posing no threat to the character of the country. The Ottoman rulers would not allow foreign citizens to purchase land, so Jews who did succeed in buying farmland had to find ways of completing their transactions through others, such as foreign consuls who extended protection to their own citizens abroad or long-settled Jews who were Ottoman citizens. These were not the conditions for an easy, dramatic increase in population. The Palestinian Arabs could continue to regard themselves as comfortably in control of the local scene; but some Arabs, usually young and less well established, did begin to think, very early, that the Jews might be on their way to becoming a power in the land and that they had to be resisted.

The Zionist pioneers who came after the nationwide wave of pogroms in Russia in 1903 caused the national confrontation in Palestine to become overt. More than thirty thousand arrived before World War I began in 1914, but it is reliably estimated that at least a third of them, and perhaps even half, did not remain. This is hardly an effective mass movement, but the men and women of this Second Aliyah came with much more ideological baggage than their predecessors. They were coming to Palestine not simply to make their own lot better. These young Zionists had chosen to come specifically to Palestine, rather than be part of the mass migration to the United States, because they held clearly defined ideas about creating a Jewish national home. They had come to the land to start the transformation of Palestine into a Jewish state. Slogans to this effect did not escape the attention of the Arabs, who intensified their battle against the Zionist endeavor. More Palestinians were uniting to stop Zionism, because they feared they were in danger of losing control of the land.

By 1914, the Palestinian leaders who seemed to be on good terms with the Zionists were increasingly keeping such sentiments to themselves. The "street" was increasingly anti-Zionist. In mid-1914, an anonymous, pointedly anti-Zionist political pamphlet was available in Jerusalem:

> Men! Do you want to be slaves and servants to people who are notorious in the world and in history? Do you wish to be slaves to the Zionists who have come to you to expel you from your country, saying that this country is theirs?

An equally eloquent, and even more bitter, expression of resistance to the Zionists was expressed by Khalil al-Sakakini, a Jerusalem radical, in his diary in February 1914:

> If the Arabs are asked by what right they possess this country (*bilad*), they would say that it is a natural part of the Arab lands. Yes, it was not the cradle of Arab civilisation—but it is not debarred from a share in it. This sacred precinct (in Jerusalem) and these schools are eloquent signs that the country is Arab and Islamic. The Arabs have settled in this country from very ancient times; and if this country is the cradle of the Jews' spirituality and the birthplace of their history, then the Arabs have another undeniable right (to Palestine), which is that they propagated their language and culture in it. (The Jews') right had died with the passage of time; our right is alive and unshakable. . . .
>
> What will the Jews do if the national feeling of

the Arab nation is aroused; how will they be able to stand up to (the Arabs)?[3]

The most self-conscious and dramatic of the counterattacks on Zionism came in 1918, even before the end of the war. The Palestinian reaction to the issuance of the Balfour Declaration in November 1917 had been uniformly negative. A year later, in November 1918, six patriotic and religious societies, joined by over one hundred individuals, sent a petition to the British military authorities in control of Palestine to denounce the Balfour Declaration. The authors of this petition asserted that they had "always sympathized profoundly with the persecuted Jews and their misfortunes in other countries. . . . There is a wide difference between this sympathy and the acceptance of such a [Jewish] nation . . . ruling over us and disposing of our affairs." A few months later, in February 1919, a meeting was held in Jerusalem of some thirty political activists from all over Palestine. The majority declared that "we consider Palestine as part of Arab Syria as it has never been separated from it at any time." In July 1919 the Syrian Congress formally opposed the creation of the Jewish commonwealth in Palestine and any effort to separate Palestine from the rest of Syria.

These attitudes were being defined in opposition to the position of Faysal, the eldest son of Hussein, the Sharif of Mecca and Medina, who was then being installed by the French as the ruler in Syria. Faysal had developed a relationship with the Zionists at the peace conference in Paris and, with a deep qualification, had agreed to accept a Jewish

state. Faysal signed an agreement in January 1919 with the
Zionist leader Chaim Weizmann in which he accepted the
aims of the Jews, providing that "the Arabs obtain their in-
dependence as demanded." Some weeks later, in March,
Faysal wrote to Felix Frankfurter, a jurist speaking for the
American Zionists:

> We feel the Arabs and Jews are cousins in race, hav-
> ing suffered similar oppressions at the hands of
> powers stronger than themselves, and by a happy
> coincidence have been able to take the first step
> toward the attainment of their national goals to-
> gether. We Arabs, especially the educated among us,
> look with the deepest sympathy on the Zionist
> movement. . . . We will wish the Jews a most hearty
> welcome home.[4]

But these often quoted documents had little effect.
Faysal was not in control of Syria even at the height of his
power in the turbulent months during which he reigned as
king in Damascus. His rule was overthrown in July 1920.
The letters between him and Weizmann and Frankfurter
represented the high point of an early movement toward
rapprochement between Arabs and the Zionists, but these
moves were essentially minor and abortive. Mainstream
Arab opinion, both outside and within Palestine, was mov-
ing toward hostility and confrontation.

The main outlines of the story of Jewish-Arab confrontation in Palestine between the two world wars has been
sketched out in the previous chapter, with special emphasis

on the despair that the Peel Commission expressed in 1937 as it contemplated the possibilities of finding accommodation between these two uncompromising groups. The Jews continued to insist on unlimited immigration as their basic right, and the Arabs continued to demand the end of this assault on their control of the country where they had long been the majority. There was no give in either position.

FAILED ATTEMPTS TO MODERATE THE CONFLICT

It is easy to multiply citations from formal documents on both sides, especially the often repeated and always vehement declarations by Arab spokesmen denouncing Zionism in all its forms. What is more interesting and revealing is what moderates in both groups were saying in the 1930s, when the armed struggle between Jews and Arabs had become continuous, overt, and murderous.

On the Arab side, the most liberal and conciliatory position was defined by George Antonius in the instantly famous book *The Arab Awakening,* published in 1938. In the last pages of his book Antonius denounced the suggestion of the Peel Commission to partition Palestine. Partition meant that the Arabs would be asked to relinquish some land to create a Jewish state. Against this, so Antonius insisted, the Arabs had only one choice, to use violence. Antonius did deplore "the terror raging in Palestine," but he added,

> The fact must be faced that the violence of the Arabs is the inevitable corollary of the moral violence done

to them, and that it is not likely to cease, whatever the brutality of the repression, unless the moral violence itself were to cease.

Antonius offered a solution he considered "beyond the smokescreen of legend and propaganda":

> There seems to be no valid reason why Palestine should not be constituted into an independent Arab state in which as many Jews as the country can hold without prejudice to its political and economic freedom would live in peace, security and dignity, and would enjoy full rights of citizenship. Such an Arab state would . . . contain provisions . . . for ensuring the safety and inviolability of the Holy Places of all faiths, for the protection of all minorities and minority rights, and for affording the Jewish community the widest freedom in the pursuit of their spiritual and cultural ideals.

For all of Antonius's eloquent language, his red lines (the lines he would never cross) were frankly stated. The solution he proposes "would protect the national rights of the Arabs in Palestine," by which he means the right to be in control of the entire country. Jews would "have a national home in the spiritual and cultural sense," but the nature of this home would be limited by the Arabs. At the end of his sketch for the future of Palestine, Antonius adds some sympathetic words for the Jews who were then suffering in Europe. Contemporary anti-Semitism was "a disgrace to its authors and to modern civilization," but the "brunt of the burden" could not be placed on Arab Palestine:

> The relief of Jewish distress caused by European persecution must be sought elsewhere than in Palestine, for the country is too small to hold a larger increase of population, and it has already borne more than its fair share. . . . To place the brunt of the burden upon Arab Palestine is a miserable evasion of the duty that lies upon the whole of the civilized world.

At his most sympathetic, Antonius was reaffirming that the land of Palestine was Arab and inalienable, that little, if any, of Palestine was available for free purchase by Jews, and that immigration had to end. The trickle of Jews who might be permitted to arrive in the future would be subject to decisions by the Arab majority. To be sure, Antonius was not proposing the expulsion of the Zionist newcomers; he was proposing instead that they be permitted only a very limited and essentially shrunken version of the national home and cultural center.[5]

Antonius's views should be compared to those of the leading political figure among the most liberal Zionists, Judah Leon Magnes. He was a Reform rabbi from the United States who had become the first president of the Hebrew University in Jerusalem. For the three decades after his arrival in Palestine in the early 1920s, Magnes was the most prominent political figure among those who wanted peace and compromise with the Arabs. He was willing to yield the dream of most Zionists for a Jewish state and even for a Jewish majority. What he could not abandon was the idea that "the Jewish people are to be in Palestine not on sufferance (as during the days of the Turks), but as a right—a right solemnly recognized by most governments and by the League of Nations, and also by thinking Arabs." Magnes insisted that three rights belonging to the Jews were "elemental and hardly to be contested":

> What is our Zionism? What does Palestine mean for us? As to what we should want here I can answer for myself in almost the same terms that I have been in the habit of using many years:
>   Immigration.
>   Settlement on the land.
>   Hebrew life and culture.[6]

These quotations are from an essay that Magnes wrote and published in English, Hebrew, and Arabic in 1930, after the Arab riots of 1929, and the immediate reaction of the British government under Prime Minister Ramsay MacDonald was to suspend Jewish immigration and land purchase in Palestine. Magnes, the pacifist and the opponent of nationalist fervor, both Jewish and Arab, weighed in with firm support for the essence of the Zionist position: that Jews had the guaranteed right in the provisions that governed the British mandate to come freely to Palestine and to buy land there. Magnes would repeat these views in the 1940s to the members of the several commissions that considered the future of Palestine, first on behalf of the British and Americans (the Anglo-American Commission of 1946) and then, the next year, on behalf of the United Nations. Magnes, the liberal, the most "pro-Arab" of all the major Jewish figures in Palestine from the 1920s through the 1940s, never stopped insisting that free immigration and the right of Jews to purchase and settle on the land were nonnegotiable.

Clearly and unmistakably, in the point-counterpoint between the views of George Antonius and Judah Leon Magnes, the issues that had been fundamentally in play for many years were restated: the Arabs, at their most amenable, would not countenance the partition of Palestine and would not accept the notion that even a minuscule Jewish state could legitimately exist in the region. Antonius deplored violence but found it understandable. What else were the Arabs to do? Without violence they had no hope of stopping the creation of a Jewish state. Magnes, the pacifist, was willing, and even eager, to surrender the trappings of statehood, but he would not give up the preambles that almost inevitably led—in the real world and not the world of his theological and cultural dreams—to a Jewish majority and to power in Jewish hands.

The battle between Jews and Arabs in Palestine had, thus, been defined in the 1930s not by firebrands and ultranationalists on both sides whose agendas were more overt and pugnacious. There was really no middle ground between the moderates, not then, and not in the next fifty years, especially after the state of Israel was proclaimed in 1948 and succeeded in defending its existence in war.

THE BITTER RESULTS OF THE WAR OF 1948–49

Informed readers of these pages probably now expect an account of the conflict between the Israelis and the Palestinians during the war of 1948–49 and in the decades after the creation of the state of Israel to the present. Such accounts, from every conceivable point of view, exist by the dozens, though few convey the profoundly angry effect of that war on both sides. In some of these books, this history is even told with objectivity—to the degree, that is, that human beings are capable of freeing themselves from their preconceptions and prejudices. But we must remember that in the hearts of Israelis and Palestinians the war and its aftermath destroyed almost all that was left of any middle ground between them. The war of 1948–49 was itself a prime example of one of the contentions in this book: that the Palestinians and their allies refused to accept the Zionist claim that Jews had a right to exist in their own independence on some part of the soil in Palestine. This point has already been made earlier in these pages, but it needs to be emphasized again: the war that the Arabs lost in 1948–49 was not a border war about the size of the two states that the United Nations had enjoined in its decision in November 1947 to divide Palestine between Jews and Arabs; it was a war to abort and destroy the nascent Jewish state. The Arabs lost their status as the majority in the land. Each side had lasting reason to be hurt, angry, and distrustful.

In the years that followed, Gamal Abdel Nasser came to power in Egypt and became a great hero in the wider Arab world by announcing again and again that he was rallying the Arabs toward a policy of utterly destroying the Zionist state. In May 1967, Nasser, the president of Egypt, made it absolutely clear that he had closed the Strait of Tiran, at the entrance to the Gulf of Aqaba, the aim being "to wipe Israel off the face of the earth and to restore the honor of the Arabs of Palestine." He urged the Arab people to fight because, as he told a press conference on May 28, 1967, "we will not accept any possibility of coexistence with Israel." The next day he spoke to the Egyptian National Assembly and predicted the great victory that awaited the Arabs: "God will surely help us and urge us to restore the situation to what it was in 1948."[7]

Nasser was not alone in this wish. In their various metamorphoses, the official representatives of the Palestinian people never wavered from this policy. The glue that has held the Palestine Liberation Organization together from the time it was founded in 1964 to the present is the desire to destroy Israel. In May of that year, 422 Palestinians from ten Arab countries met in Jerusalem (that is, in the eastern part of the city, which was then held by Jordan), announced the creation of the Palestine Liberation Organization, and ratified the charter of principles for which it stood. The key provisions of this document were

ARTICLE 1. Palestine, within the boundaries it had during the period of the British Mandate, is an indivisible territorial unit.

ARTICLE 6. Palestinians are those Arab citizens who, until 1947, had normally resided in Palestine, regardless of whether they have been evicted from it or have stayed in it. Anyone born after that date of a Palestinian father, whether inside Palestine or outside it, is also a Palestinian.

ARTICLE 17. The partition of Palestine in 1947 and the establishment of Israel are entirely illegal, regardless of the passage of time, because they were contrary to the will of the Palestinian people and its natural right in its homeland, and inconsistent with the general principles embodied in the Charter of the United Nations, particularly the right of self-determination.[8]

This position did not change after the Arab defeat in the Six-Day War in 1967, and it has remained the announced program of the PLO into the 1990s. The purpose of the Palestinian national movement was the destruction of Israel and the return of all the Arab refugees to their homes, which had been made uninhabitable by the state of Israel. Such a return could happen only if there was a mass expulsion of the Jews.

To be sure, Edward Said, the American professor who was beginning to emerge in the 1960s as the spokesman in the West for the Palestinians, did not seem to take such a hard-line view. He wrote an essay in the winter 1969 issue of *Columbia Forum* in which he pleaded for "a more inclusive (rhythm of life), the Palestinian, which had before 1948 allowed Christians, Muslims and Jews to live in counterpoint with each other." Said was, of course, conveniently forgetting that this "counterpoint" had become armed warfare in the decade or so before 1948. But it was no doubt useful to forget such facts in order to suggest that the situation ought to return to earlier times before the partition of Palestine by the United Nations in 1947, which Said did not mention, and the loss by the Arabs of two full-scale wars in 1948 and 1967 in which they had tried to destroy the state of Israel.

THE ISRAELIS RESPOND TO THE ARAB HARD-LINE

Israeli governments were not always preoccupied with combating the Palestinians' vow to destroy Israel or their insistence that all the refugees from the war of 1948–49 return to their original homes. The up-front response by the Israelis was that they were busy building up their state and they were certain the Palestinians could not succeed in destroying them. Nonetheless, from the very beginning of the Zionist enterprise, the Palestinian question had never ceased being central in the minds of Israel's strategic thinkers. Their views ranged from the conviction of Hashomer Hatzair (the "Young Guard"), the most left-wing of the Zionist parties, that a binational state be established in Israel, to the view of Yosef Weitz, a leader of the effort to acquire and cultivate more land for Jewish settlements. In 1940, influenced by the hostility of the guerrilla warfare with the Arabs between 1936 and 1939, Weitz wrote the following:

> It must be clear that there is no room for both peoples in this country. . . . If the Arabs leave the country, it will be broad and wide open for us. And if the

Arabs stay, the country will remain narrow and miserable. . . . The only solution is Eretz Israel [the land],
or at least Western Eretz Israel, without Arabs. There
is no room for compromise on this point.[9]

The mainstream position was neither the binationalist
theory of Hashomer Hatzair nor the angry, maximalist opinion of Yosef Weitz. It was best defined by Chaim Weizmann,
who insisted that the key to the future for Jews in Palestine
required

> genuine friendship and cooperation with the Arabs
> to open the Near East for Jewish initiative. Palestine
> must be built without violating the legitimate inter-
> ests of the Arabs. Not a hair on their heads shall
> be touched. The Zionist Congress . . . has to learn
> the truth that Palestine is not Rhodesia, and that
> 600,000 Arabs live there, who, before the sense of
> justice of the world, have exactly the same right to
> their homes in Palestine as we have to our National
> Home.[10]

On the Arab side, no one responded to such invitations,
and from the Jewish side the offer of friendship was not,
generally, as warm and generous as Weizmann's words im-
plied. Since 1949 the treatment by Israel of the Arab minority within its borders was far less generous than it should
have been. Not even the most committed partisans of Israel
can take much pride in this record. I do not know whether

total equality for the Arab citizens of Israel would have fundamentally helped reduce the acrimony of the Israeli-Palestinian conflict, but one of the tragedies of this history is that it was never tried.

In the early years, right after the conclusion of the armistices that ended the war of 1948-49, the Israelis attempted to move on toward a permanent settlement with the Arabs, but they were essentially rebuffed. At several points in the next decades, Israel reopened the question, but the result was the same. The Palestinians themselves wanted no settlement with Israel. They preferred to keep reminding world opinion that most of them were miserable refugees from their land.

In those decades some Israeli leaders thought that the existing Arab governments, or at least several of them, might be persuaded to take the lead in tempering the intransigence of the Palestinians. Perhaps if enough aid was offered, these countries would agree to absorb hundreds of thousands of the Palestinian refugees, or some of these refugees might choose to go west and make new lives for themselves. Indeed, during the first forty years of the existence of the state, Israel kept looking for an Arab partner who could be induced to take over the bulk of the Palestinian refugees. The trouble with this dream is that it could not be put into effect. No Arab state wanted to take in a substantial number of Palestinian refugees—especially if such action would help Israel solve a troubling problem.

Throughout the first three decades of its existence, Israel was eager to solve an even more fundamental problem.

It kept looking for Arabs who would acknowledge that the Jewish state had the right to exist in the Middle East. This hope was the underlying motive of Israel's announced policy after the Six-Day War. It was waiting to "trade land for peace"; that is, it would return the lands, or most of them, that it had conquered in the Six-Day War to Arab authorities if they would make peace and extend formal recognition to Israel. The prime minister of Israel, Levi Eshkol, said openly, several times, that he was waiting for a phone call from the Arabs. To be sure, some Palestinian notables wanted to make peace with Israel, but the effort was blocked by General Moshe Dayan, who insisted that the only peace worth having had to be made with the "legitimate Arab states." No phone call ever came. On the contrary, Arab representatives met on September 1, 1967, in Khartoum and announced that their policy toward Israel was no recognition, no peace, and no negotiation.

The first dramatic breakthrough came ten years later with a bid from Egypt's president, Anwar Sadat. Sadat decided to fly to Jerusalem in mid-November 1977 to speak to Israel's parliament, the Knesset. Sadat was the first Arab head of state to come to Israel since its beginning, and he made it very clear that he was prepared to recognize Israel's legitimacy and to use his best efforts to lead the Arab world, and especially the Palestinians, toward peace with Israel. In his speech Sadat laid down the conditions: a Palestinian state was to be created in the West Bank, and all of the territories Israel had conquered in the 1967 war were to be given back, including East Jerusalem.

Arthur Hertzberg

THE AMERICANS INTERVENE AND ARE
ASKED BACK AGAIN AND AGAIN

Sadat's dramatic visit was not followed immediately by negotiations between him and the new prime minister of Israel, Menachem Begin, but the Americans under Jimmy Carter had become heavily involved in what they saw as a major chance to make an end of Jewish-Arab hostilities. Much of the next year was spent on diplomatic maneuvers by both the Israelis and the Egyptians, so Jimmy Carter finally lost patience. He decided to invite both Begin and Sadat to be his guests at Camp David, so that all three of the principal participants would be in the same place. The meeting began on September 5, 1979, and lasted far longer than anyone expected. By the seventeenth day and after the seemingly total collapse of the negotiations two days earlier, an agreement was arrived at. Jimmy Carter euphorically announced it as the framework of peace in the Middle East, but Carter was far too optimistic. The Camp David negotiations had produced a great breakthrough; it represented an important change in Jewish-Arab confrontation, but it was not yet a foundation for complete peace.

In the deal that was hammered out at Camp David, the terms of Israel's phased withdrawal from all of the Sinai Peninsula were very precisely defined and exact dates were given for its various stages. To be sure, an equally elaborate protocol announced the objective of creating a Palestinian state, beginning with the limitation of further Israeli settlements in the captured land of the West Bank; but this protocol amounted to a pious hope by the Egyptians rather than a contract between them and the state of Israel. That there was no real connection between these two deals that were supposedly made at Camp David soon became apparent. Menachem Begin insisted that there was no understanding at Camp David that would limit his efforts to found new Jewish settlements in the West Bank. However, Egypt did not respond that Begin was in breach of contract. The Egyptians knew full well that if they took such an action, the return of the Sinai Peninsula would halt and they would, therefore, lose the basic gain they expected from making peace with Israel and recognizing its existence.

The critics of Egypt in the Arab world were proved right. Sadat had entered the negotiations to get his land back and not to be troubled by the Palestinians. Begin had been willing to make the deal at Camp David because the Sinai Peninsula had not been part of biblical Israel, and he therefore had no ideological reason for wanting to hold on to this territory. The Egyptians had never demonstrated great fondness for the Palestinians, the very people they had kept part of under arrest in Gaza from 1948 to 1967, when they ruled and administered that territory.

Right after Camp David it was not in the interest of either power to let the truth about their deal come out and so I, for one, found myself more unpopular than usual in both Israeli and Egyptian circles. I told the truth about the Israeli-Egyptian peace treaty, based on what I had heard in Cairo during a visit in 1980. It was no surprise to me that I had some trouble getting an essay published in which I described the political atmosphere in Cairo that summer, but the editors of the *New York Review of Books* agreed to print my hardheaded and not very complimentary description of the origins and meaning of the Camp David agreement.[11]

We need to understand what Israel did and did not get from this deal. First of all, it did achieve a resounding triumph on the question of diplomatic recognition. The largest Arab state, Egypt, had made formal peace and exchanged ambassadors. Never mind that this peace soon turned out to be formal and cold; it was an act of recognition by the leader of the Arab world. Second, unfortunately, Egypt had made absolutely no commitment to help solve the question of the Arab refugees. It had only promised that it would not bother the Israelis much with pressure to let three to four million refugees return to the land of Israel. The question of what to do with these people continued to haunt Israel even after the dramatic events at Camp David in 1979.

ISRAELI AND PALESTINIANS REMAIN AT WAR EVEN AS THEY TRY TO FIND ACCOMMODATION

The prime representative of the refugee issue was the PLO. It had been created and continued to exist as the voice of those who harbored the grievance that the Israelis had seized their country. The base of the PLO became southern Lebanon, the area contiguous with the northern border of Israel. In the 1970s this region was essentially under the control of the main political-military component of the PLO, the Fatah, and occasional attacks were launched at Israeli towns and habitations, but these attacks were not the basic problem.

The basic problem for Israel was that the PLO was behaving in southern Lebanon as a quasi-government. This Israel could not countenance. The habit of self-government by the Palestinians might spread and become a force with which everyone else in the neighborhood would have to deal.

Contingency plans were drawn up by Israel's general staff to put an end to the presence and power of the PLO. In 1982, an attack was launched in an operation called "Peace for the Galilee." The announced objective of this endeavor was to force the PLO to move 45 kilometers back from the border so that its missiles could not reach Israel. The trouble with the mantra about "peace for the Galilee" was that it was simply not true. General Ariel Sharon, who was then the defense minister in Menachem Begin's Cabinet, had misled his own government. He ordered the troops to go as far north as possible, at the very least to Beirut. Sharon's military triumph would force the Palestinians out of Lebanon, and he hoped to install Israel's Christian allies in power there. Israel would thus have a friendly government in the north that would be, at the very least, a partial satellite. This dream was not attainable because Sharon's favorite Christian ally, Bashir Gemayel, although formally elected president of Lebanon, was assassinated almost immediately thereafter.

Much more damaging were the events in the refugee camps of Sabra and Shatilla, which housed Palestinians in the area of Beirut. While Israeli troops looked on, Gemayel's Falange militia massacred several hundred Palestinian men, women, and children (the exact number has remained in dispute). No one doubted that this was a dreadful event. There were immediate protests all over the world, but the most impressive of all was the largest demonstration that had ever been held in Israel. On the Saturday night after the massacre, central Tel Aviv was jammed with four hundred thousand people who came from all over the country in protest against Israel's military leadership. The immediate result of the outcries within Israel itself was the appointment of an investigating commission chaired by the chief justice of the Supreme Court, Yitzhak Kahan. A few months later, when the results of this inquiry were made public, blame was widely apportioned, but the most pointed conclusion was the demand that the defense minister, General Sharon, be forbidden to continue in that office. He did leave the ministry, but he remained in another post in Menachem Begin's coalition Cabinet. In that new position Sharon busied himself with spreading new settlements into the middle of the West Bank.

The military and political result of Israel's excursion into Lebanon was the expulsion of Yasir Arafat and the PLO from that country. During the summer and fall of 1982, the PLO leadership made its last stand in the port area of Beirut, under constant bombardment from Israeli guns placed on a ridge overlooking the port. The American government, under Ronald Reagan, decided to rescue Arafat and his followers. They were taken offshore and moved across the Mediterranean to Tunis, which offered hospitality to the PLO on the condition that whatever political or military action it might carry out should take place inside or along the borders of Palestine.

For the next decade the PLO in Tunis continued to represent the cause of the Palestinian refugees. However, its leaders had been in exile so long that they no longer knew the younger element who had grown up after 1948 in the West Bank and Gaza. A new element that was native to the land was arising to contest leadership of the Palestinian cause, that is, the cause of the Palestinians who had never left the land and were now living under Israeli control. To be sure, Arafat was the recognized leader of the Palestinian people. A fair amount of lip service and even some sincere devotion were expressed toward him by Palestinians in the West Bank, but it was an open secret that he was not really in control there. The acts of resistance to Israeli rule, which kept increasing, were almost all homegrown.

Arafat kept himself in the political foreground by traveling all over the world to remain the visible symbol of Palestinian nationhood. On the matter of Palestinian identity, most Israelis had come to agree with Arafat. They had long given up on former prime minister Golda Meir's repeated proclamations in the late 1960s and early 1970s that there were no Palestinians, only Arabs who happened to live in the territory that was once governed by Great Britain under a mandate from the League of Nations. But Arafat had become a political fact on the international scene. He had been recognized by well over a hundred governments; within the United Nations he was treated as a head of state. Arafat and the PLO—that is, the Palestinian national cause—simply could not be ignored.

Radical thinkers in Israeli governing circles came up with a new and daring idea. If Israel had been seeking, from the very beginning of its existence, a settlement with the Arabs that would recognize its legitimacy, why not deal with Arafat?

This idea became even more radical when the question of the Palestinian refugees was added to it. Why should Israel not offer Arafat a Palestinian state in the West Bank and Gaza and, in effect, ask him to trade in the cause of the refugees for his accession to the presidency of a state on its own land?

This was the grand design, and so a deal was made in 1993 in Oslo, with the help of the Norwegian government: Yasir Arafat and the entire leadership of the PLO could come to the West Bank and install themselves as the heads of a functioning Palestinian Authority. The exact boundaries of the land that this quasi-Palestinian government would control would grow by stages. A final settlement of all the questions between Israel and this Palestinian body would be negotiated within three to five years. At the end, there would be two states between the Mediterranean and the Jordan River living in peace and substantial economic symbiosis with each other.

The Oslo Agreement was at first hailed with enthusiasm, and not only in Israeli and Palestinian circles. It seemed to offer the promise of an end to the long-standing quarrel between Israeli Jews and Palestinian Arabs, but these hopes were not realized. On the Israeli side, powerful forces representing the settlers on the West Bank and their sympathizers opposed the creation of a Palestinian state. They knew that many of the new Jewish settlements would have to be evacuated, and they did not trust a Palestinian state to police the factions within its own borders that would continue to be intent on destroying Israel.

The single greatest attack in Israel on the Oslo Agreement happened in November 1995 when Yigal Amir, a right-wing religious ideologue, shot Prime Minister Yitzhak Rabin dead as he was leaving the platform one night at a large peace rally in Tel Aviv. The assassin and those who admired him were certain that they were doing God's work; they were representing the true interests of the Jewish nation by shooting down the prime minister who had agreed in Oslo to help the Palestinians create a state of their own.

On the Palestinian side, an *intifada* ["uprising"] had broken out some years earlier, in November 1987, to express Palestinian frustration at Israel's continuing to increase settlements and tighten its grip on the occupied territories. The immediate cause for this outbreak was a traffic incident near Ashkelon in which four Palestinians had been killed and six wounded. This *intifada*, consisting mostly of stone throwers, lasted four to six years. It was superseded by the hopes that were aroused by the negotiations in Oslo. These negotiations seemed to promise a Palestinian state as the successor to the Palestinian Authority created in 1993 under Yasir Arafat.

By the year 2000 these hopes were fading, and in September a second *intifada* started in which guns and bullets replaced stones and rocks as Arab weapons. This escalation was, supposedly, a response to a provocation by Ariel Sharon, who was then running for prime minister. He came in state to the Temple Mount, which seemed to suggest some Israeli expansionist designs in this most sensitive of all places. But it has been proved that the second *intifada* was prepared and even begun before Sharon's theatrical appearance at the Temple Mount. The Palestinian Arabs were going to war against the Israelis, who, the Arabs felt, were not implementing the Oslo Agreement because they wanted the peace negotiations to become dormant and fail.

It is possible to search the literature and find that in the 1980s and especially the 1990s Jews and Arabs—and on occasion Western governments in Europe and concerned Arab governments in the Middle East, such as Hosni Mubarak's Egypt—kept coming up with peace plans to try to bring the conflict to an end. At various points there were even draft positions announced by the PLO that accepted the existence of the state of Israel, provided a Palestinian state was allowed to arise in all of the Arab-held territory that Israel did not control before the Six-Day War began. The trouble with all these plans was that the more intransigent groups among the Palestinians refused to accept any peace plan that gave formal recognition to the existence of Israel.

To be sure, Arafat himself had softened on the question of the existence of the state of Israel, and he had even gone as far as to express his willingness to let the question of the refugees be settled "reasonably" according to United Nations Resolution 194. This document, which had been enacted in December 1948, had not specified the number of refugees who were to return; it simply agreed that if they so willed, they could return, on the assumption that only handfuls would want to go back and all the rest would accept resettlement or compensation. But most of the Palestinian Arabs did not attach themselves to any compromise. They said, instead, that Jews had no place in their Palestine—exactly what their predecessors had been saying for one hundred years.

THE FATE OF ZIONISM

CAN THE PALESTINIANS AND ISRAELIS MAKE PEACE BY THEMSELVES?

One should not give the impression that nothing has changed in recent years. On the contrary, on both sides of the conflict there has been some dissent from the dominant position. In the Jewish camp, post-Zionism has now become evident among some Israeli intellectuals and their supporters in the Jewish diaspora. The burden of their song is that Israel should indeed become a normal nation by adopting the principle of making no distinction between Jewish inhabitants and the Arabs who live among them as citizens of the state. The most striking contention of the post-Zionist position is that Israel's law of return, which grants the absolute and unquestioned right to move to Israel and assume citizenship to any Jew who wants to come to the country, should be repealed. Henceforth, so the argument goes, everyone who wants to immigrate to Israel, no matter who he or she may be, should be subject to the same rules.

This post-Zionism, however, has made very little impact in Israel and in world Jewry. Zionists did not come to Palestine more than a century ago in order to establish a Western-style, nonethnic republic. The sacrifices that made the state of Israel possible were evoked by the vision of a Jewish state engaged in fashioning a contemporary Jewish society. Chaim Weizmann said it best in one of his greatest speeches, when he appeared before a committee of the General Assembly of the United Nations in 1946. He rejected the suggestion that the Jewish national home be established as a minority presence within an Arab state: "Those of us who made our homes in Palestine did not do so with the object of becoming Arab citizens of the Jewish persuasion."[12] It is self-evident that the kind of state and society envisaged by post-Zionists would evoke little loyalty in the Jewish world as a whole.

On the Arab side as well, there has been some movement away from the "first principle" that the Jewish presence in Palestine is never to be accepted as legitimate, no matter what arguments might be made on its behalf. A few prominent Palestinians have acknowledged as a fact that Zionists are in Palestine to stay and that the state of Israel is hardly likely to collapse. The most recent major figure to espouse this view in public is Sari Nusseibeh, president of Al-Quds University in Jerusalem, who has even served for a year or so as the formally designated representative of Yasir Arafat and the PLO in Jerusalem. Nusseibeh does understand that the Jews' claim to Palestine is based on a long history of regarding themselves as exiles since the destruction of the Second Temple in the year 70; they have never accepted the notion that they could settle down permanently to live an adequate Jewish life "singing the song of the Lord on foreign soil." In a speech at a conference of the Washington Institute in October 2002, Nusseibeh has even taken the bold step of suggesting that those Palestinian refugees who want to return to their homeland should return not to Israel, but to the Palestinian state to be created. Nusseibeh added that "the Palestinian state should be demilitarized." In his view, this would serve the interests not only of the Israelis, but also of the Palestinians.

The recognition of the Jewish claims in Palestine can also be found in the writing and thought of an Arab intellectual of substantial aristocratic lineage, George Hourani. He wrote as early as 1968 that Jewish and Palestinian claims to the land were radically different in character and yet each had a validity of its own. He concluded his analysis by asserting, "The logic of partition is the same today as it was under the British Mandate, the previous period of forced marriage. Both parties want to be in Palestine, but they are not there for love of each other; the driving force of both is to lead their own lives in freedom from each other. Both are happier with a whole half (of Palestine) than with sharing the whole."[13] For years thereafter, George Hourani was ostracized in the Arab world for having accepted the existence of Israel. Just a few months before he published this "heresy," the Arab League had met in Khartoum and reacted to the Israeli victory in the Six-Day War by announcing that there could be no peace with Israel, no negotiation, and no acceptance of Israel's right to exist. That remained for many years the seemingly unshakable conviction of the PLO. Israel was not to be recognized; it was to be destroyed.

The most sophisticated version of this Arab first principle—that Israel should cease to be—was pronounced in the West by Edward Said. He began to agitate in the 1980s for the complete integration of all the land between the Mediterranean and the Jordan River, provided that the enlarged state would guarantee the voting rights of every one of its individual citizens. That would have immediately meant that the enlarged Israel would have contained a population that was more than 40 percent Arab. Given the comparative birth rate of Jews and Arabs (Arab families had more than twice as many children as Jewish families), the

Arabs would become the majority within a couple of decades or perhaps even sooner. This suggestion seemed tempting, but it never became the demand of the PLO. This is an uncomfortable fact that Said managed not to know in his book, *The Question of Palestine,* which was published in 1979. The announced position of the PLO had remained its call for the destruction of Israel with scant suggestion that many Jews would be welcome to remain in Palestine.

When it appeared, Said's book was widely praised even by such figures as Anthony Lewis, a *New York Times* columnist and a leader of liberal opinion, "as a compelling call for identity and justice." What Said had written was, at best, a personal call by Said himself; it did not represent the Palestinian resistance movement. It had not come forth, as Said asserted that it had, as

> an idea and a vision for the Middle East that broke sharply with all past ideas. This was the idea of a secular democratic state in Palestine for Arabs and Jews. Even though it has become almost a habit to deride this idea, there can be no serious way of minimizing its tremendous importance. . . .
>
> The ghetto state, the national security state, the minority government, were to be transcended by a secular democratic polity, in which communities would be accommodated to one another for the greater good of the whole.[14]

Said's prose could be read, as indeed it was by some Western liberals, as a call for détente between the combatants, but translated into Arabic—not necessarily the language, but certainly the mentality of the warriors—Said was read as pointing the way, as George Antonius had done earlier in 1938, toward the creation of a state dominated by Palestinians, which would make an end of Israel. Said's book used rhetoric to describe the seemingly good and beautiful revamped state of Israel in which people would be transformed into peaceful, cooperative beings as they enjoyed their individual rights. One could perhaps think such thoughts in a moment of reverie in New York or London or Oxford, but this was wildly untrue to the real situation on the ground in the Middle East. The Palestinian purpose remained the destruction of the state of Israel, and Said's vision provided a seemingly elegant way of accomplishing this purpose.

All this changed radically in 1993 when Israel invited Arafat and the PLO back into the territories that Israel controlled and began to negotiate with Arafat for what his share would be in the governance and control of parts of historical Palestine. Though this momentous change was covered with many fig leaves of rhetoric and by declarations about solving the whole of the Palestinian question, including that of refugees, Arafat was essentially agreeing to change roles. He would look toward becoming the first president of a new state of Palestine, that is, of the Arabs who had remained in the land, and he would de facto abandon being the leader of the refugees—but Arafat could never quite do it. He seemed to have his own deepest roots in the PLO's historic role as champion of the undivided land of Palestine, and he also remained under unrelenting pressure. Radical and warlike Palestinian factions kept igniting and feeding the fires of war between

Jews and Palestinians. Arafat and the political figures in his orbit had to keep asserting their loyalty to the cause of the refugees and, of course, the continuing demand for nothing less than all of Palestine. Again, in the 1990s, under radically different political circumstances, the leadership of the Palestinian Arabs was behaving—or being forced to behave—as it had throughout the twentieth century.

But there had to be some softening of the Arab and Palestinian positions. Arafat knew that a Palestinian state could not be achieved even by the tactics that were being used in the second *intifada,* which had begun in 2000, that is, by the use of guns rather than stones by the Palestinian resistance to the Israelis. It was necessary to persuade the majority of Israelis, and of course the government of the United States, that Israel would be better off if a Palestinian state were created in the West Bank and Gaza. A major move toward a changed policy was taken in the spring of 2002 at a meeting of the Arab League in Beirut. Israel was offered peace if it would acquiesce in the matter of a sovereign Palestinian state and agree to negotiate with the Arabs a "reasonable conclusion" to the question of the refugees from the 1948-49 war. But this declaration did not send the Israelis on a stampede to Riyadh in Saudi Arabia, where this proposal had first been outlined, or to Washington, to ask the American president forthwith to assemble the relevant diplomatic teams at Camp David to negotiate the peace arrangements.

The Israelis thought that the Beirut declaration was a public-relations gesture that would dissolve into smoke and recriminations across a negotiating table. Israelis of all political persuasions knew that the Arab right of return evoked, as well, the greatest passions among the Palestinians: they demanded that they be allowed to return to their homes of fifty or sixty years ago, and many still had the keys for these houses in their pockets. But the Israelis knew that the Arabs could not go home again. The land and its buildings had mostly changed beyond recognition. And the situation had become tenser since 1967, as the Israelis had built settlements and dwelling places for at least a quarter of a million Jews in the West Bank and in Gaza.

The folly of the Israeli "creeping annexation" of the West Bank has been that it created among the Palestinians an even more enraged grievance against the Israelis. The official Israeli position in the immediate aftermath of the Six-Day War in June 1967 was to keep offering to "trade land for peace." At the very beginning, that slogan was not entirely specified. Eshkol's cabinet had decided in secret to trade the Sinai Peninsula and the Golan Heights for peace, but it never offered the West Bank and Gaza. These cabinet decisions made no difference because the Arab world—including especially the Palestinians—had answered in Khartoum in September 1967 that there could never be peace and recognition of this usurper state, even if it returned all the conquered territories. The door was thus open for expansionist forces in Israel. The reigning justification in the early years of the creation of settlements in the West Bank and even in Gaza was that this building activity would force the Arabs to sue for peace. That assertion was, and remains, a delusion. On the contrary, the consequent narrowing and relative impoverishment of the Palestinian presence in the West Bank has fueled more anger and more violence on both sides.

The most enraging element in the unabating drive for increased settlement has been the increasing dominance of a religious motif among the Jews who have justified and hailed these actions. It is the "will of God" that the Jews occupy the "undivided land of Israel." Religious fervor has expressed itself in great anger at long-standing hurts. Orthodox Jews had for many, many centuries avoided ascending the Temple Mount because its soil remained holy and was not to be stepped on by individuals in a state of impurity, but others, especially those who belonged to the religious Zionists, had long felt that the Muslims in control had no right to exclude them, and certainly not now, after 1967, when the mountain was under Israeli military control.

As we have seen above in this chapter, Jews had for many centuries been excluded from entering the mosque in Hebron that had been built over the graves of the patriarchs and matriarchs; Jews were grudgingly permitted to ascend the first seven steps of a staircase that led to the shrine but were in immediate danger of bodily harm, or worse, if they dared go farther. By Passover of 1968, a group of religious zealots arranged to spend the holiday in rented rooms in a hotel in order to pray at this very holy shrine. The military government of Hebron agreed to receive them and protect them, but when the holiday was over, these temporary worshipers refused to leave. The Israeli government, then under a prime minister of the Labor Party, Levi Eshkol, did not have the political courage to order the army to remove them.

Thus, one of the results of the Six-Day War was the creation of lasting religious friction, both in Jerusalem and in Hebron, as well as in several less religiously important places.

This was, of course, only the beginning of the story of Jewish settlement in the territories the Israeli army had conquered in 1967. In the past thirty years, the Jewish population beyond the green line (the border of Israel as it was defined in the armistice agreements of 1949–50) has grown from negligible numbers to at least two hundred and fifty thousand. About two-thirds of this population live right across the former border in new neighborhoods that are indistinguishable from greater Jerusalem or from the suburbs on the outskirts of Tel Aviv. The other one-third inhabit settlements scattered all over the West Bank and in several places in Gaza. The most exact count now, in 2003, is that these Jewish towns and villages control half of the land of the West Bank and even more of its water resources. This means that Arab agriculture is increasingly parched. There is very little pretense that the ongoing creation of such settlements (the process has not stopped regardless of who has been in control of the Israeli government) will make the creation of a Palestinian state in the West Bank ever more difficult. It would require major uprooting of Jewish settlements. Such action would cause civil disobedience or even some armed rebellion among Jews.

The new shooting began some weeks before Sharon showed up in state in the Arab quarter of the Old City of Jerusalem. The new *intifada* and all its violence is a contemporary expression of the embittered and lasting quarrel between Jews and Arabs in Palestine. As the Israeli grip on more and more of the land seemed to become permanent and irreversible, Arabs turned to what seemed to them to be their only option, violence. The Arabs hoped that they could scare many Jews out of the land—but that had been tried many times before and failed. The Israeli government shot back, ever more vehemently, by targeting every Arab militant it could find, but more security has not emerged at the point of a gun. And so, a century of hostilities has continued.

SO WHAT ARE THE POLITICAL RESULTS?

It is tempting to say that the Israelis and the Palestinians remain, after a century of conflict, with only two legacies: each remembers its hurts and will not give up these memories. One could then proceed to the assertion that the road to peace must lead the Israelis and the Palestinians to take account of each other's pain. They must make peace because they have no ultimate choice; they must accommodate each other in a land that neither will leave. This accommodation can take place only if each side is willing to let its history recede into the past as it looks forward to the benefits of a more peaceful future.

The trouble with this vision is that it is not true. It cannot be realized unless other major interests in this conflict either agree to be helpful or accept their exclusion. To begin with the Israeli side, the security and political position of the state are inconceivable, at the present, without the support of the United States. This means that American government policies in the Middle East are a major influence on the direction that Israel takes. It makes a vast difference whether the administration in Washington is essentially permissive of the creeping annexation of the West Bank or whether it makes a serious effort to stop it. In May 2003, the Bush government decided to take the lead in pushing both the Israelis and the Palestinians toward implementing the "road map," the peace plan that it helped devise together with Russia, the European Union, and the United Nations. One of the central requirements of these proposals is that the Israelis stop increasing the size of existing settlements and, as a first step, remove all the new settlements that were established after the middle of 2001. After some hesitation, Prime Minister Sharon announced his adherence to the plan, but he made it apparent that he was reluctant to accept the rigors of the road map on the question of settlements. A freeze on their expansion and a rollback on some that exist will cause deep political trouble in Israel. It will not go smoothly.

On the Palestinian side, the situation seems more complicated, but it really is not. To be sure, several European countries support the cause of Palestinian nationalism in the battle with the Israelis, but despite all the noise they are making, they are, ultimately, forces of secondary importance. They can send the Palestinian Authority money and make speeches at the United Nations, but the European nations do not have the power to determine the future of this conflict. The fundamental issue for the Palestinians is not attracting positive statements or cheering visits from European dignitaries. It is the matter of the long-standing policy of violence. Here too the government of the United States is now actively involved. It has told the new prime minister of the Palestinian Authority, Mahmoud Abbas, that he must stop the violence. He has been asked to acquire legitimacy in American eyes by repressing, with all the firepower at his disposal, the Palestinian militants in their several factions. This task is not likely to be accomplished very soon. It will probably take a long time for the hostilities to end, or nearly to end—but the ending of the *intifada* is not the only problem that confronts the Palestinians.

They must also change their relationship to the rest of the Arab world. The cause of a free Palestine (not usually distinguished from the demand for the destruction of Israel) and for the unlimited return of Palestinian refugees to their former homes inside Israel seems to be the mantra of the Arab "street" in most Muslim countries, especially those in the neighborhood of Palestine. But how believable is the Arab street? Has the Palestinian question really become the flash point in a clash of civilizations between America and Israel on the one side and the whole of the Arab world on the other?

There are two reasons to doubt this image of Middle Eastern politics. The first is the well-known fact that the Palestinians have remained unpopular in large parts of the Arab world. When the Egyptians were in control of Gaza, from 1949 to 1967, they would rarely allow the Arabs of Gaza to travel to Egypt even for brief sojourns. The first result of the victory in 1991 that freed Kuwait from rule by Iraq was the total expulsion of two hundred and fifty thousand Palestinians who were then the bulk of Kuwait's workforce. By the same token, the Saudi government pays handsomely, in words and treasure, to keep the most militant Palestinians from thinking about subverting its autocratic regime and to keep al-Qaeda from making trouble in the homeland of Osama bin Laden and many of his supporters and followers. It is now evident that these policies are not doing the Saudis much good. They are now reeling under direct attack from the one or the other of the Arab terrorist groups.

There is a subtext to the pan-Arab outcry of "Let the Palestinians go back to their homes." It is the not very well hidden further assertion "and let them leave our neighborhoods." Therefore, if there is to be a sorting out of the political interests in the Middle East that shadow the Israeli-Palestinian conflict, the true relationship of the Arab world to the Palestinians has to be dealt with in candor. It then might be discovered that the real nub of the issue is that the Arab world as a whole prefers to keep the question of the Palestinian refugees unresolved because it refuses to integrate any more Palestinians into its various countries—and the anger of the Arab street directed at Israel helps to deflect and obscure some of the deeper anger in the various Arab societies.

Perhaps the most fundamental of all the questions is that both Zionist and Palestinian nationalism have not really come to terms with their roots in religion. The critics of Israel keep accusing it of being dominated by the rabbis. This is simply not true. Israel is by far the most secular and Western of all the states in the Middle East. Israel's fundamentalists and messianists are too prominent these days, but they are minorities that do not dominate Israel's society, even if their influence on the settlement movement is strident and harmful. The far deeper problem is with the Palestinians. To be sure, Palestinian nationalism began as a secular movement, but it has been nearly transformed by the religious fervors that have been growing in contemporary Islam. Israeli and Palestinian nationalisms can come to peace with each other—even to some semblance of coexistence—only if they both accept the modest aims of secular nationalism.

FOUR

◇◇◇◇◇◇◇◇◇◇

WHAT MANY LIBERALS
CAN'T SEE

At this moment in the history of the Jewish-Arab quarrel, large elements of the Western liberal intelligentsia have joined the battle on the side of the Palestinians. They are acting out a psychodrama of their own: for the first time in many centuries Jews have power, and many of the leaders of Western opinion do not know how to deal with Jews when they are not victims, especially since such Jews remind them of the Holocaust, when six million Jews were murdered by the Nazis and their helpers while the bulk of the European intelligentsia remained silent. To be sure, Israel's policies since 1967 have contributed to the present stalemate. The Israeli government has attempted to suppress armed rebellion by the Palestinians by escalations of force. Nonetheless, the scathing critiques of Israel are essentially irrelevant. It is not within the power of those who write and read these attacks on Israel to help make peace.

The situation is becoming worse because Arab and Jewish protagonists in the armed battle, and even some American Christians who support the policies of the right wing in Israel, are stoking the furnace in the name of their religious certainties. So long as the issue keeps being redefined as a question of finding ways to do to the will of God in blood and fire, the possibility remains that the Middle East may well explode into chemical, biological, or nuclear war. The liberal ideologues, among whom are many who would like to destroy Israel, and the Jewish hard-liners, who would like to make the Palestinian Arabs miserable enough to leave the land, are both incapable of making peace between them. But is peace possible?

In the present controversy between the Zionists, who created the state of Israel, and the Palestinians, who are affronted by Israel's existence, much of the rhetoric has become inflammatory. On the Zionist Israeli side, it has become all too convenient to label every critic of Israel an anti-Semite. It is equally convenient for the critics of Israel to charge the Zionists with the unforgivable sin of colonialism. This conflict has always involved deep passions: thus, many on each side have persuaded themselves that their opponents are on the side of Satan. The fight has become as vitriolic as the assaults in the seventeenth century on witches or heretics. How can one compromise with anti-Semites or colonialists, especially when so many seemingly respectable pundits and journalists are now urging their readers not to forgive such sinners?

I am able to understand the Palestinians and their partisans in the Arab world much more easily than I can fathom the motives of those Westerners who are hostile to Israel. The Israelis and the Palestinians are engaged in a struggle that will determine their future and the future of their descendants. It is all too human for them to get carried away and engage in unbridled rhetoric, even though some or even many on both sides know that when the shooting war ends, they will have to learn to talk about, and to, each other in more peaceful language. What I cannot fathom is the amount of passion—and venom—that Western intellectuals of various political factions and many of the political left are displaying in this conflict. These are people who pride themselves on their universalist concerns. Is the battle between Palestinians and Israelis really the worst outrage that exists today in the world? To rebut such an idea, I need not mention some other armed conflicts. It is enough to be reminded of the vast disaster of AIDS in Africa, of the death by neglect that awaits at least forty million people, to make the point that a truly universalist outlook would not put the battle between the Israelis and Palestinians at the top of the moral agenda.

More immediately, is it really true, as the enemies and critics of Israel would have it, that the hostility between the Israelis and the Palestinians is the most painful and bloodiest conflict afflicting the Arab world? These self-proclaimed purists of human rights seem not to have noticed that Saddam Hussein, while he was in power in Iraq, massacred at least three hundred thousand Arabs, Kurds, and Iranians. His neighbor, President Hafez Assad of Syria, slaughtered uncounted tens of thousands. These outrages are simply not mentioned; they were semi-ignored when they happened and soon forgotten by those who say they speak for human rights. So what explains the near hysteria now in parts of the West over the existence of the Zionist state in a corner of the Arab world?

The source of Arabs' anger is that they are at war with the Jews. The source of the anger in the West is that the Western liberals and leftists are at war with themselves. They have been struggling to define a new attitude toward Jews and Judaism since the beginning of the modern era, and they have failed. Some of the evidence of this struggle is bizarre. To cite just one example: many Western intellectuals pretend not to know that almost every Arab state is, by its own definition, a Muslim state, a theocracy, but Israel is regularly lambasted as a state governed by rabbis. This is a strange accusation when everyone knows, or should know, that since Israel's founding all but one of its prime ministers have lived secular lives and all have led essentially secular governments.

THE "JEWISH QUESTION" IN MODERN TIMES

We shall not understand Western reactions to the Israeli-Palestinian encounter in recent years unless we go back to the basic change in Western Jews' and Christians' perceptions of each other at the beginning of the modern era. Until the sixteenth and seventeenth centuries the relation between Christians and Jews was understood in theological terms. Because Christianity was the dominant religion, the faith of the majority, Jews were allowed only enough room to survive in lowly occupations, such as peddling, or in high-risk ones, such as banking, but they had little economic or social mobility. In their attitude toward Jews, Christians could choose between contempt and tolerance, but most had no doubt that Jews deserved their low, and precarious, place in society. They merited the punishment that society inflicted on them as the followers of a "superseded religion."

In the modern era, however, new questions appeared. How could one proclaim that "all men are created equal" and not make room for equality of rights and opportunities for all the citizens of the realm, believers and unbelievers alike. To be sure, some of the most prominent of the thinkers who defined modernity, such as Voltaire, kept insisting that society would endanger itself if it conferred equality on all Jews. Voltaire insisted that the Jews were by nature an antisocial tribe, but the main thrust of the Enlightenment in the eighteenth century was to teach that, at their very worst, Jews were the hardest to reform of all the people who had been debased by persecution. Yet even Jews could be redeemed by a proper Western education, which would cure them of the superstitions they had learned from the Talmud. Above all, these unfortunates needed radical change in the social conditions in which they lived. So, by the first half of the nineteenth century the dominant opinion seemed to have become that what would be good for Jews, and for society as a whole, would be to open the doors wide for Jews to assimilate and to disappear as a community.[1]

But that larger society was not really hospitable to those Jews who had done its bidding and assimilated. In Germany, even though Jews were supposedly equal citizens of the united empire after 1870, they were kept out of high office in the army and the civil service. Almost no one of Jewish origin, except converts to Christianity, was ever appointed to an academic post at one of the universities. The situation was somewhat better in nineteenth-century France and a bit better still in Great Britain, but there was enough discrimination against Jews everywhere to keep the Jewish question very uncomfortably alive.

The greatest shock to the cliché that in modern times anti-Semitism was becoming a memory from the nasty past came in the Nazi era. The Holocaust, the murder of six million or more Jews by the Nazis and their collaborators—and by the many millions in Europe who knew what was happening and kept silent—was the climactic act in modern times of the encounter between Jews and the majority society. At the end of World War II, Western society had no choice but to acknowledge guilt and be silent in shame, but this did not come easily to some of the intelligentsia. Some began to offer explanations in which the Jews were told they had brought this disaster upon themselves. Others busied themselves as early as the 1940s and 1950s with explaining, with the help of some Jewish scholars, that Nazism was a creation of the gutter of modern society and that the great European traditions did not share in the guilt. As the years went by, these apologists avoided the innumerable studies proving that ordinary, respectable bourgeois knew about and profited from the murder of the Jews, often participating in these outrages. Hitler's architect, Albert Speer, was certainly not from the gutter. On the contrary, he was a cultured German of a good family, but he was the major proponent of using slave labor in producing weapons for the German army (he worked most of the laborers to death).

The decisive turn in relation to the Jews took place in the mid-1940s. Those who survived after six million Jews had been murdered in the Holocaust were visible in displaced persons camps. One hundred thousand or more of these homeless people could not go back to their former dwellings in central and eastern Europe. Their homes had been confiscated and local anti-Semites prevented them from reclaiming what was once theirs. At this time also the Western powers, led by the United States, were busy demobilizing millions of soldiers. No country was eager to open its doors wide to refugees. Westerners of conscience agreed in 1946 and 1947 that these refugees required help but "nimby," that is, "not in my backyard." The ultimate result was an agreement at the United Nations that Palestine should forthwith admit these one hundred thousand refugees. Great Britain balked, preferring to give up the mandate to govern Palestine, which it had held since 1920. Some months later, in November 1947, the UN General Assembly ruled that the land should be divided, permanently, into two states, one Jewish, one Arab.

The reaction of the Arabs was that the West was solving its problem of bad conscience about the Nazi years and its present unwillingness to stretch toward accommodation of the survivors at the expense of the Arabs in Palestine. The Jews responded by saying essentially, "So what?" Had not the Grand Mufti of Jerusalem joined the Nazis? Had not the Arabs sat out the war? Most important, even Martin Buber, the moral leader of those Jews who were most concerned about fair treatment for the Arabs, recognized in those very days there could be no justice for the Jews without some injustice and discomfort for the Arabs of Palestine. This was inherent in the realities of the human condition, but the Jews were owed a home of their own. As they were achieving their national hope, the only thing within the Jews' power, Buber insisted, was to do as little harm as possible.

The Jews got their state within three years of the end of World War II, but the Holocaust and its aftermath left not very well hidden resentment in the hearts and minds of much of the European intelligentsia. They bitterly resented being told by Jews, over and over again, that they were guilty of large-scale, passive collaboration with the Nazi murderers or indifference to the murders. The Jews simply could not be allowed to maintain the moral superiority they had conferred upon themselves as the ultimate victims of the Nazis. The "revenge" would come when the Jews, or at least some of them, could be put in the gun sights of Western indignation and accused of having used the Holocaust to make themselves into the "new Nazis."

The very state of Israel, which had seemingly been created as recompense for the past, began to be enlisted as proof that Jews shared a universal tendency to abuse power and to demean, despoil, and even murder their enemies. To be sure, in some of the battles between Jews and Arabs in Palestine, the new possessors of power, Israelis with guns, did commit the excesses that power had made possible. During the war of 1948–49, there was a massacre involving more than a hundred deaths at the Arab village of Dir Yasein, on the outskirts of Jerusalem, but it was noteworthy that those who conducted this action were widely condemned in Israel and in the Jewish world as a whole. I do not want to be misunderstood as suggesting that in the armed struggle for the creation of Israel Jews behaved as holy angels. On the contrary, this was a fierce war. But not even the most partisan of Arab historians has ever suggested that Jews ascended to power by conducting large-scale murder of those whom they regarded as their enemies.

Yet the facts were less important than the radical change in the relationship between Jews and non-Jews. Even after the creation of the state of Israel, Jews still thought of themselves as victims, as an endangered people that had barely survived and that had been coming back to life after a tremendous trauma. But to outsiders Israel appeared to be a growing political, economic, and military power, the dominant state in the Middle East. This opinion became all the more fixed as Israel moved into the orbit of American protection, in large part because of the growing influence of Jewish citizens in the public life of the United States. As early as the 1950s and certainly in the immediate aftermath of the Six-Day War in June 1967, the critics and enemies of Israel tried to paint the Jewish state as behaving toward its opponents, the Palestinians, as the Nazis had once behaved toward the Jews. This equation was totally untrue. Most of those who made this accusation even knew that it was a conscious lie. Under the Nazis the Jewish population of Europe had decreased, through the mass murder of more than six million Jews, by at least two-thirds; under the Israelis, during the more than thirty years of their occupation of the West Bank and Gaza, the Arab population had doubled. No one denies that much injustice was done to the Palestinians, but to equate the conduct of Israel with that of Nazi Germany is ludicrous. But it was a great relief for some Western intellectuals to proclaim this lie. The act of comparing Israeli generals to Nazi generals seemed to pardon those who had not resisted the Nazis.

THE LEFTIST DISTEMPER WITH ISRAEL

A personal confession: the most wearying and upsetting task in writing this book has been having to read and assess many vehemently anti-Zionist documents, but I have had no choice. These attacks must be confronted and answered.

One of the most extreme attacks I have read appeared in England as a short article, titled "Israel Simply Has No Right to Exist," in the *Guardian* on January 3, 2001. Its author, Faisal Bodi, was identified only as a Muslim journalist. Bodi's essential assertion was that "Israel should not exist." To this he added that "the sympathy evoked by the Holocaust was a very handy cover for Israeli atrocities." These assertions were a fact that he had "always considered central to any genuine peace formula." Bodi went on to argue that the only reason for the existence of Israel is the clinging by the Jews to the promise in the Bible that "unto thy seed I have given this land," but this promise does not obligate the Palestinians. No supposed leader of the Palestinians can ever compromise with the Israelis on behalf of his exiled and occupied people. Bodi is therefore free to denounce anything that Israel does to suppress armed attacks on its population, but the assaults by suicide bombers and armed infiltrators against Israeli citizens need not be mentioned at all. Has not an aggrieved nation the right to push intruders off of its land? Those who kill Jews "are heroes and martyrs"; the Israelis who kill Palestinians are "evildoers who are behaving with an arrogance which institutionalizes the inferiority of other people and generates atrocities against them with alarming regularity." Bodi's solution is to suggest the creation of one state dominated by Palestinian Arabs in which "Jews will continue to live in the Holy Land . . . as equals alongside its other rightful inhabitants." He predicts that after Israel is willing to attest to the illegitimacy of its existence and dismantle itself, it "can expect that the Palestinians will be forgiving and magnanimous in return."

I read this essay, not with astonishment that a Muslim journalist could think such thoughts, but with disgust at the editors of the *Guardian*. Bodi's views are not much more extreme than the continuing line of the *Guardian*'s policy to this day: Israel is always wrong because its very existence is illegitimate. But is Israel really less legitimate than the United States, which exists on land on which Native Americans lived in the seventeenth century? Are the editors of the *Guardian* prepared to maintain that their colleagues at the *New York Times* should surrender their offices and take boats back to the lands of their ancestors so that the Native Americans who once roamed the island now known as Manhattan could occupy the Times Building and establish a newspaper of their own?

To be sure, the arrival of the Zionists in Palestine came two and a half centuries later, under different historical circumstances, but it was at least as legitimate as the invasion of the mouth of the Hudson River by the Dutch, and soon the English, in the seventeenth century. The explanations for colonization that have been conventionally advanced emphasize Europe's need in the seventeenth and eighteenth centuries for more room for its growing population and the desire of persecuted groups, such as the Puritans who came to New England, for a chance to begin a new life in the New World. The supposedly civilized and educated editors of the *Guardian* (I wonder how many of them graduated with firsts in history at Oxford or Cambridge?) know these considerations very well, but they forget them when they contemplate the state of Israel. What right did Jews have to flee czarist mobs and Nazis and find a home in which to try to rebuild their culture and refresh their traditions?

The editors of the *Guardian* are not alone in their position among the British intelligentsia. In the spring of 2002 Tom Paulin, a lecturer at Hertford College, Oxford, was quoted in an interview he gave an Egyptian newspaper, *Al-Ahram,* as saying that the Jewish settlers in the West Bank and Gaza "should be shot dead. I think they are Nazis, racists. I feel nothing but hatred for them." This outburst was based on the premise that he had never believed that "Israel had the right to exist at all." Paulin added that he had "resigned from the Labor Party because Tony Blair's government was a Zionist government."

This line of denunciation of Israel inevitably and invariably moves on to the next assertion that Israel cannot be held to account, that is, it cannot be made to dismantle itself as a Jewish state, because it is supported by the United

States. To be utterly blunt, American support is vastly important for Israel, but it is not its last line of defense or the sole bulwark of the survival of the state. On the contrary, the strength of Israel was created and exists to this day because the vision of modern Zionism has been realized in Israel. From right to left, all the Zionists—from Judah Magnes and Martin Buber, who preached peace and reconciliation, to Vladimir Jabotinsky and Menachem Begin, who wanted Zionism to achieve maximum national power—insisted that the new Jews they were creating had to be able to defend themselves and their people. Israel continues to exist in the world because it has taken great care to be the dominant military power in its region and because, as all the world knows, it possesses sufficient nuclear capability to make the cost of trying to push it into the sea unbearable to its enemies. Those who hate Israel and wish its destruction must always remember that they cannot win through newspaper editorials what they have never been able to achieve on the battlefield. Make no mistake: even the doves and the liberals in the Jewish community, even Jews like me who have been opposed to the creeping annexation of the West Bank since it began in the late 1960s, will never make common cause with those who want to put an end to the Zionist state.

And yet the connection between America and Israel remains important, both to the Zionists and to their enemies. The anger that it evokes in Europe is even more vehement on the Continent, especially in France, than it is in Britain. To be sure, the British left is very angry with the Labor prime minister, Tony Blair, for being allied with the United States. On the British satirical stage, he has been repeatedly portrayed as George Bush's poodle. But even though British majority public opinion did not support Blair's choice to participate with the Americans in the war in Iraq, it is not as bitter as opinion in France. The difference is that alliance with the United States, the "special relationship," is largely accepted in the United Kingdom as the continuing basis for its role of consequence in international affairs. Without the American connection, the British would have nowhere else to go but toward Europe, where they could easily be swamped in the affairs of the Continent by the dominant power of the Germans and the French together, most often aided by the Russians.

The French, on the other hand, have never made peace with the notion that they are permanently a secondary power. Since the days of de Gaulle they have imagined themselves a counterweight to the United States in the leadership of Europe. Never mind past gratitude for American help in World War I and for American predominance in the victory that liberated France from the Nazis in World War II. Politics is, in the mind of the realists at the top of the French government (almost any French government), about real and immediate interests—and in regard to these interests those realists are determined not to be dominated by the Americans or pushed by Tony Blair to behave as a more docile ally of Washington.

One finds almost everywhere in contemporary French writing vehement attacks on the Americans from both the right and the left. When George W. Bush visited Paris on May 26, 2002, a variety of anti-American and pro-Palestinian protesters demonstrated against him. They carried slogans calling Bush a criminal and denouncing Bush and Sharon together as "assassins" and as the "real terrorists." Many of the demonstrators did not represent schools of thought within the French political spectrum. They were from the suburbs, where the four or five million recent immigrants to France, the Muslims of Algeria and the rest of North Africa, live. At the Bastille, a small group of demonstrators burned American and Israeli flags. French newspapers reporting this event were, or said they were, embarrassed by the hatred of Jews that had been on view in this demonstration. Nonetheless, a few months later in its issue of May 28, 2002, *Le Monde* essentially accepted the basic accusation that "Zionism equals racism." The counterattacks on the enemies of Israel were described as strengthening the racists' stereotype "in order to attach to the Arabs or the Palestinians a stigma," which is, of course, "intolerable" because it is against human equality. It follows, therefore, according to *Le Monde*'s logic, that the battle against Zionism and the state of Israel is part of the battle for universal human rights.[2] There is, of course, no mention in this article of the human right of Jews to go safely to a Passover seder in Netanya or a pizza parlor in Jerusalem and not be murdered by suicide bombers.

The statement summarizing the attacks on Israel was published by a Muslim who lives and works in France, Mohamed Ennacer Latrèche, on July 1, 2001. His pamphlet was distributed some time later at a conference in Strasbourg on April 9, 2002, on the theme "Anti-Semitism, racism, xenophobia, intolerance, questions that concern us all." Latrèche's basic assertion was that Israel is absolutely illegitimate and that it is a criminal entity: "Israel is a colonial state. . . . By becoming the murderer of children, the Zionists have unmasked themselves before the world. . . . Apartheid, racism, and exclusion are parts of its foundation. Terrorism, destruction, manipulation, and defamation are its tools of action. . . . Zionism, like Nazism, will disappear sooner or later."[3]

The basic premise of Latrèche's pamphlet is that Israel is a colonial state and, therefore, it must be removed and completely destroyed. This theme is more prominent in French attacks on Israel because Algeria's independence in 1962 and the emigration of many hundreds of thousands of settlers from that troubled land are still very much a part of immediate memory in France. It follows, from this history, that once a state is declared to be colonialist, anything that state does to defend its citizens is considered an unforgivable assault on human rights. By this standard, Israeli children who are killed by suicide bombers are colonial intruders; Arab children who are shot while throwing stones at Israelis are martyrs and heroes. But what if the Jews were never colonialists (as I have maintained above) but rather refugees running for their lives? Is it still in order to kill them whenever possible? Is it morally acceptable to slaughter these Zionists or their children or grandchildren? Is this a cause that should engage those who pronounce themselves to be defenders of human rights?

The fury of the Zionist state's enemies becomes fiercer when they contemplate the power of the "Jewish lobby" in the United States. Israel's critics brush aside the possibility that the United States is most comfortable with Israel because it is rooted in the same democratic values that are the very essence of the American tradition. Those who would denounce Israel dare not remember that every Arab state is, without exception, an autocracy or a dictatorship. Even to those who do not know Israel at all well, it is clear beyond doubt that freedom of speech, sharp debate, and uncompromising criticism are the bread and butter of Israel's daily life. The critics of Israel almost never mention the quality of Israel's internal life because, at the very least, it would force them to explain why Arab societies are essentially repressive.

The enemies of Israel prefer to insist that Israel is important to the United States because the American Jews dominate American politics. They admit that Jews represent perhaps 2 percent of America's total population, but point out that Jews are more often found to be donors to political campaigns, activists in the debates on American policy, especially in foreign affairs, and members of the intellectual and academic elites. I plead guilty to all these charges. But I ask, "So what?" Such complaints fit every other minority. Political influence reflects not only numbers but also economic power. In American affairs, the oil lobby is perhaps the most powerful of all the special interest groups. At this moment, various organizations representing Arab Americans are rising in visibility. The respectable and hardworking Arab men and women who came to America to advance their personal fortunes are contrasting themselves to the radical Muslims who want to make war on all those who stand in the way of their version of the will of Allah. These American organizations have been rapidly rising to public notice not simply because they are saying what the American people want to hear, that

Muslims in this country are obeying the laws of the land. The undercurrent in these declarations by American Muslims is that they are in the process of becoming a force in American public affairs. Their votes may not yet be able to determine a national election, but that day may yet arrive.

We are, therefore, facing a paradox. American oil barons protect their interests and those of their Arab partners who own the oil of the Middle East. Several other ethnic minorities in America, such as African Americans, defend their political positions, but how dare the Jews in America speak up about the future and the safety of Israel? I have quarrels with much of what the Jewish lobby keeps saying; it has usually been even more hard-line than the government of Israel itself. I have not been alone in denouncing the Jewish intransigents, both in Israel and America, but I must ask one more question of Israel's critics: Do you really want to destroy Israel? Are you convinced that if this does happen, it will usher in a new age of freedom and peace in the Middle East? Are you sure that the Arab factions will find so much joy in uniting to destroy Israel that they will then stop murdering each other?

THE ASSAULTS ON THE UNITED STATES

After reading many, many pages of attacks on the connection between Israel and the United States, I have been forced to conclude that the underlying enemy is not even Israel, the much maligned Zionist state, but the United States of America. These attacks are not being constructed to persuade the

United States to abandon its commitment to Israel. On the contrary, Israel is being portrayed as both the henchman and the evil counselor of America, which is only too eager to accept its partnership and advice. Among Israel's critics, this distinction has been made most clearly by Noam Chomsky. In a speech he gave in Boston on December 14, 2000, in the early months of the *intifada* that had begun at the end of August of that year, Chomsky maintained that

> Arab opinion . . . claims that the United States overlooks Israeli terrorism because of the Jewish influence or Jewish lobby, or something like that. And this is simply untrue. It's missing the fact that a much more general principle applies to this case and to many others. The principle is that the United States has the right of terrorism and that right is inherited by its clients, and it doesn't matter who they are. So, Israel happens to be a U.S. client, so it inherits the right of terror.[4]

I cannot refrain from adding that the more I read of Noam Chomsky, the more intolerable I find his pathological hatred of the United States. To be sure, it is one of the glories of American democracy that he has remained a professor in a leading American university and that he has enjoyed the right to free speech guaranteed by the Constitution of the United States.

I do not want to suggest, by citing the paragraph above from Chomsky's December 2000 lecture, that all of his ire was directed at the United States. In answer to questions that day, Chomsky insisted that the "overwhelming mass of the atrocities" in the war between Israel and the Palestinians "are by Israel and the United States." It is the United States that provides the military helicopters with which the Israelis carry out "ninety percent of the atrocities." In order to emphasize the sins of Israel, Chomsky went on to assert, citing no evidence in support, that "in 1967 Israel was not attacked and no one even pretends that." His assertion is, of course, simply not true. Was it Israel, and not Egypt, that asked in May 1967 for the United Nations peacekeepers on the borders between Israel and Gaza to be withdrawn? Was it Israel, and not the blustering president of Egypt, Abdel Gamal Nasser, who closed the Straits of Tiran?

Chomsky's attitude is not entirely shared by the Palestinians. They still have some hopes of breaching the alliance between the United States and Israel, if only the Arab oil powers would agree to put enough economic and political pressure on the Americans. European liberals, and especially those of the European left, do not think this way. For them America is exactly what the propagandists of fundamentalist Islam describe it to be: the "great Satan." Fundamentalist Islam, the faith of many Arabs, and secular universalism, the doctrine of the liberal left in Europe, are radically different movements, but they both want to undercut and end the status of the United States as the world's one superpower.

One of the great debates these days is about the relationship between the West and Islam. Is a clash of civilizations inevitable? The answer is not clear or certain. It depends on whether Islam is conquered in the next few decades by its militants or whether it is tempered by religious moderation.

There can be no doubt that some lessening of the tension between Palestinians and Israelis would make a major difference. Many of those who criticize Israel and maintain that its conduct is the cause of the present impasse know that they cannot simply declare Israel to be a pariah. They know that it will not disappear. The enemies of Israel—at least some of them—know that they will have to find some path to détente between the combatants.

One of the interesting attempts to push this line, with some finesse, has been made by Tony Judt, a liberal who proudly describes his own Zionist past. Judt is a professor of modern European history at New York University. Writing on May 9, 2002, under the title "The Road to Nowhere," in the New York Review of Books, Judt pronounces that "the solution of the Israel-Palestine conflict is . . . in plain sight. Israel exists. The Palestinians and other Arabs will eventually accept this; many already do." But why is Tony Judt so certain that the creation of a Palestinian state on "nearly all of the occupied territory" will bring a settlement? That offer was basically put on the table by Ehud Barak, who risked and lost his control of Israel's government when the settlement that he suggested was rejected out of hand by the Palestinians. The parties supposedly got closer in a meeting at Taba in January 2001, in the last days of the Clinton administration, but the Palestinians refused to accept the more generous arrangements that were being negotiated. The evidence of the entire history of this conflict is against Judt's cavalier presumption that the Palestinians will eventually accept such a deal. Various versions of a two-state solution have been offered to them since the 1930s, but they have always refused to accept them.

The basic thrust of Judt's essay is hostility to the Israelis. He argues that if they would only accept the hard choices they have to make, to dismantle the settlements and to return almost all of the land of the West Bank and Gaza, all would quickly be settled—but this is nonsense. Any careful historian and observer of contemporary political affairs, especially in the Middle East, knows that the Israelis, when polled, have consistently voted by a majority of two to one to endure the substantial pain involved in the return of land and the removal of settlements if this would achieve peace with the Palestinians. The polls among the Palestinians have continued to show a majority for continuing the struggle; the ultimate objective of the Palestinians is the end of the state of Israel.

It is convenient, as Judt does in his essay, to blame Sharon and the Israeli political establishment—not to mention "the country's liberal intelligentsia who Pilate-like have washed their hands of responsibility." Judt asserts that all of them together, "are chiefly to blame for the present crisis, but they are not alone precisely because the Israelis assumed that they have a blank check from Washington. The United States is willy-nilly a party to this mess." Judt heaps the blame on the Bush administration for its sympathy with Israeli hardliners. This is a very useful debater's tactic, but that is all it is. One can attack Sharon and Bush to the applause of one's fellow liberals without having to deal with the hard question: So what would happen if the Palestinians were confronted with their own hard choice, to recognize Israel and give up the dream of swamping it with refugees returning from the camps? Let us imagine that the Palestinians do agree that the refugees be admitted to their own new state of Palestine, in the West Bank and Gaza. Can a Palestinian regime police the thousands of angry people who will come to Palestine looking for ways to infiltrate Israel?

But these are not the only problems with Judt's essay. He rests his case on the example of Algeria, where the French were finally persuaded to do the reasonable thing and withdraw (insinuation: Zionism is colonialism), and on South Africa, where the white minority handed the government over to the blacks (further insinuation: Zionism is racism). Judt seems to use these two cases to imply what Israel ought to be doing: the Israelis should follow these rational examples and agree to be a minority in an Arab Palestine, or they should simply go home to the places from which they came; but Judt knows better than to make this suggestion overtly. He knows that the Israelis will not leave. No doubt, enough of the Zionist is left in him from his earlier life to cause him to remember that the Zionist state is indeed a special case. Its claim to existence is based on Jews' historic connection to the land and on their fears for their survival in this dangerous and murderous time. So today, as many times before in the past hundred years, we must again ask the as yet unanswered question (which Judt has avoided): How are the Palestinians and their supporters, both among the Arabs and the liberal left, going to be persuaded to accept this upsetting anomaly, the Jewish state?

There are two themes upon which almost all the critics of Israel vehemently agree. Israel is too close to the Americans, and Israel uses American arms, such as attack helicopters, unfairly in its war against Palestinian militants. The first is an old argument recycled. Throughout the days of the British mandate in Palestine the Zionists were accused, over and over again, of existing in the land because the British favored them. The Arab enemies of Zionism have always been certain that if Jews were left to fight out this quarrel unaided by Great Britain in the 1920s or by the United States in recent decades, the Arabs would win. But is this true? In the Zionist Yishuv, the Jewish immigrants to Palestine after 1882 defended themselves with no help from the Ottomans and after 1929 with almost none from the British. In 1967 the Israelis won against all their enemies in the region without any help from any other power. Throughout its existence Israel has always made a great point of maintaining military superiority over all its Arab enemies combined.

It can even be argued, in reverse, that it is the Palestinians who are the greater beneficiaries of foreign arms and foreign help. There is some manufacturing of weapons in the West Bank, but most of the arms that the Palestinians use to assault Israel are smuggled in, mostly from Lebanon and Egypt, and then distributed among the various networks of fighters who keep the region unstable. It is even more true that foreign money is central to the survival of the Palestinian resistance movements. Here the relatively few millions raised from Arabs abroad are of minor importance. What is central to the story are the subsidies given directly to Hamas, the Islamic Jihad, the Hezbollah, and the PLO itself by Iraq (before the fall of Saddam Hussein), Saudi Arabia, and Iran. Granted that an attack helicopter is a deadly weapon, but is the promise of a large check from Iraq or Saudi Arabia to the family of a suicide bomber substantially less culpable? This largess is an enticement to murder. And yet, in his frequent discussions of the Israeli-Palestinian quarrel, the most famous and most quoted debater on these issues in the past thirty or forty years, Noam Chomsky, keeps condemning the armaments that Israel gets from America and pays little, and all too dismissive, attention to the havoc that suicide bombers have inflicted on Israeli citizens. In the essay published at the end of October 2000 largely to attack the policies of the United States, Chomsky does admit that Israel has not invented its tough response to those who endanger its citizens:

> Israel is employing official U.S. doctrine, known here as "the Powell doctrine," though it is of far more ancient vintage, tracing back centuries: use massive force in response to any perceived threat. Official Israeli doctrine allows "the full use of weapons against anyone who endangers lives and especially at anyone who shoots at our forces or at Israelis," according to Israeli military legal adviser Daniel Reisner. . . . "We cannot second-guess an Israeli commander who calls in a Cobra (helicopter) gunship because his troops are under attack," another U.S. official said. Accordingly, such killing machines must be provided in an unceasing flow.[5]

This argument was advanced also by Edward Said, writing in the weekly *Al-Ahram Online* (April 18–24, 2002), under the title "What Israel Has Done":

> And still Sharon makes the case that Israel is struggling to survive against Palestinian terrorism. Is there anything more grotesque than this claim, even as this deranged killer of Arabs send his F-16s, his attack helicopters and hundreds of tanks against unarmed people without any defense at all? . . . As popular protests grow worldwide, the organized Zionist counter-response has been to complain that anti-Semitism is on the rise.

Does Edward Said really believe that the Palestinians have no way of fighting back? Where do the snipers and the suicide bombers come from? Who has been creating the underground factories for bombs and weapons?

One could go on quoting various aspects of the assault on Israel in its angriest and indeed most hysterical forms. To give some examples, the press in Greece contains such nuggets as calling Israel a "Nazi country" and condemning its attacks on "defenseless Palestinians." The Jews of Greece are criticized for "not taking a stand against the genocide of the Palestinian people by Sharon." On April 1, 2002, a large caricature was published on the front page of one of the Greek dailies under the title "Holocaust Two." The drawing was of a Israeli soldier in Nazi uniform aiming his rifle at a Palestinian who was dressed in the striped clothes of the inmates of Nazi concentration camps. In Manchester that spring, Professor Mona Baker, an Egyptian-born professor, fired two Israeli scholars from the boards of two academic journals she publishes because they are Israelis. Dr. Baker's reason was that she was breaking totally with Israel: "Many of us would like to talk about it as some kind of Holocaust, which the world will eventually wake up to, much too late, of course, as they did with the last one." In the United States, at Harvard University, calls were issued by some groups for the university to disinvest in Israel. Lawrence Summers, the president of the university, was strongly against this suggestion and that effort ended.

ARE THERE SOLUTIONS?

But, putting aside those who want to see Israel as the new Nazi state for psychological reasons of their own (which I described in the opening pages of this chapter), it is possible to make some sense out of the less hysterical critiques of Israel and the solutions to the Israeli-Palestinian war that they propose. Chomsky, Judt, and Said each seem to want to return to their youth, real or imagined, because they remember that there was, then, a more hopeful future for the region. As a teenager Chomsky was in the circle of adherents of the Zionist group Hashomer Hatzair. Its central orientations were on the creation in Palestine of a socialist Zionist community and being the vanguard of Jewish-Arab cooperation to create a binational state. For a number of years in the 1950s, Chomsky and his wife wanted to move to a kibbutz in Israel, and they did, in fact, spend six weeks in 1952 at the collective farming community Hazorea, where Chomsky seems ruefully to have discovered that he was not cut out for the innumerable hours of physical labor that farming required.

But Chomsky has never given up a lifelong obsession with Israel/Palestine. His response to Zionist critics has been, repeatedly, that he is neither an enemy nor an outsider. He is simply the representative of one of the old Zionist traditions, socialist binationalism, which he made his own in his youngest years. Writing in the 1970s, Chomsky still imagined that one could build this golden utopia even though international socialism is now barely alive and too much has happened between Jews and Palestinians for them to be able to slip easily into living in peace with one another:

It seems to me not impossible that after the experience of building and living in new Montenegros and Lithuanias, Jews and Arabs may turn to a better way, one which has always been a possibility. It will be based on the fundamental principle, already cited, "that whatever the number of the two peoples may be, no people shall dominate the other or be subject to the government of the other." Each people will have the right to participate in self-governing national institutions. Any individual will be free to live where he wants, to be free from religious control, to define himself as a Jew, an Arab, or something else, and to live accordingly. People will be united by bonds other than their identification as Jews or Arabs (or lack of any such identification). This society, in the former Palestine, should permit all Palestinians the right of return, along with Jews who wish to find their place in this national homeland. All oppressive or discriminatory structures should be dismantled, and discriminatory practices should be condemned rather than reinforced. The society will not be a Jewish state or an Arab state, but rather a democratic multinational society.[6]

Twenty years later Chomsky reluctantly found himself to be more sober and less hopeful. Writing in the introduction of a new book, *Middle East Illusions* (2003), Chomsky contemplated the possibility of a two-state solution, but rejected it:

While a settlement along the lines of the Rogers Plan and the UN resolution might bring stability, I believe that it will perpetuate conditions that have prevented the realization of the just hopes and highest ideals expressed within each of the warring societies. In a Jewish state, *"klein aber mein"* ["small, but mine"], there can be no full recognition of basic human rights, and at best, only limited progress toward a just society. Such limitations are inherent in the concept of a Jewish state that also contains non-Jewish citizens. A Palestinian counterpart, founded on bitterness, frustration, and despair and dominated by its neighbors, will be a mirror-image, perhaps even a distorted image. Both will be subject to reactionary forces within and domination from outside.[7]

The only hope in the long run is to realize the vision of a binational state, the dream of Chomsky's youth and that of a number of redoubtable Zionist figures in the 1930s.

Tony Judt is somewhat younger and so his direct experience of Israeli life dates to the mid-1960s. At that point, before and immediately after the Six-Day War, the thinking of Jewish liberals was rooted in the vision of realizing the partition of Palestine, of a Jewish and a Palestinian state living side by side in peace and cooperation. I am not at all surprised that, after Judt attacked Israel for supposedly being the sole culprit in creating the present hatreds, he returns to the presumption of his youth: the Palestinians will be satisfied with a state of their own in which they will live happily ever after. Such problems as refugees and the economic and military relationships to Israel will not be troubling. But the realist within me cannot avoid asking both Chomsky and Judt, who seem to yearn for the dreams of their teens and early twenties, "Where are the snows of yesteryear?"

The only one who seems to have made some progress in his thinking, with the passing of the years, is Edward Said. He has apparently finally arrived at a rather unhappy acceptance of the partition of Palestine. When he began his career as a principal spokesman for the Palestinians in the English-speaking world, Said was, as we have seen, a proponent of the creation of an Arab Palestine, which he was sure would treat a Jewish minority with generosity of spirit. More than twenty years later, in 2002, he wrote a flaming reaction to an Israeli incursion in force into Jenin, an important Palestinian city in the West Bank. In the course of fierce fighting, including the bulldozing of some buildings by the Israeli army, over fifty people were killed. The Israelis maintained that these were militants; that is, that the Israeli army had used force against those who were shooting at them. The Palestinians maintained that these were unarmed civilians, including women and children, and that underneath the rubble, hundreds upon hundreds of bodies were present: the Israelis had committed an unparalleled massacre. This version of events was soon denied by independent observers, including the representatives of the International Red Cross, but the inflammatory story was widely believed in the Arab world. Edward Said believed that a massacre had taken place and reacted with fury:

> There are reported to be hundreds buried in the rubble, which Israeli bulldozers began heaping over the camp's ruins after the fighting ended. Are Palestinian civilian men, women and children no more than rats or cockroaches that can be attacked and killed in the thousands without so much as a word of compassion or in their defense?[8]

This was classic Said. On the basis of speculation he built a mountain of indignation. When the reports proved false, Said chose not to correct his view; rather he left his insults and insinuations in circulation. Yet for all his sloganizing abilities, Said is capable of being realistic.

But Said no longer calls for a unitary state in Palestine. He knows that if the Palestinians are not to lose all of Palestine, they must accept the partition of the land into two states. Said makes no secret of his hatred for Israel—not merely for Sharon and his followers, but for Israel as a whole—but he knows that it will continue to exist:

> The profound question facing Israel and its people is this: Is it willing to assume the rights and obligations of being a country like any other, and forswear the kind of impossible colonial assertions for which Sharon and his parents and soldiers have been fighting since day one? In 1948 Palestinians lost 78 percent of Palestine. In 1967 they lost the remaining 22 percent. Now the international community must lay upon Israel the obligation to accept the principle of real, as opposed to functional, partition, and to accept the principle of limiting Israel's extraterritorial claims, those absurd, biblically based pretensions and laws that have so far allowed it to override another people. Why is that kind of fundamentalism unquestioningly tolerated? But so far all we hear is that Palestinians must give up violence and condemn terror. Is nothing substantive ever demanded of Israel, and can it go on doing what it has without a thought for the consequences? This is the real question of its existence, whether it can exist as a state like all others, or must always be above the constraints and duties of other states. The record is not reassuring.[9]

From various directions a consensus seems to be emerging: the Israeli-Palestinian conflict can be settled by the parties accepting, whether in anger or with some relief, a two-state solution. There is even some growing agreement between Israeli moderates such as Ephraim Sneh, who has held the post of Israel's governor of the West Bank, and Sari Nusseibeh, who was Arafat's representative in Jerusalem until he was fired in 2002 not long after he had been appointed.

Ephraim Sneh, writing on May 6, 2002, in *The Christian Science Monitor,* under the title "A Different Peace Plan for Israel," suggested a peace plan based on a two-state solution. The permanent borders between the Israeli and Palestinian states would not be far different from the crossfire lines that had existed on the eve of the 1967 war, with some exchange of territory to enable Israel to retain the settlement blocks that are close to its borders. In Jerusalem, he accepted the division of the city so that the Arab neighborhoods of East Jerusalem would revert to Palestinian sovereignty. "The holy basin, the old part of Jerusalem where sacred sites of three religions are located, would enjoy a Vatican-like status with freedom of access guaranteed to all faiths." The boldest part of this plan is Sneh's suggestion that the Palestinian refugees would "have the right to immigrate to the Palestinian state, but not to the Jewish state." Sneh's position is almost exactly the same as the one Sari Nusseibeh would express in Washington a few months later. Thus, one can begin to imagine, as some on both sides seem to be agreeing, that the road to a settlement between Palestinians and Jews leads to a two-state solution.

Unfortunately, these suggestions, which seem bold and decisive and a giant step toward peace, are nonstarters. The difficulty with these seemingly reasonable suggestions is that they offer no convincing solution to some harsh political realities. Let us imagine that a Palestinian state in the West Bank and Gaza is actually created within the next several years and Arafat has even retired out of politics or "ascended" to some ceremonial role of little power. Will his successors in the PLO manage to keep their new state in the West Bank free of terrorists and guerrillas who will continue to harass Israel?

I find it personally painful to have come to the conclusion I've reached because I have for many years, at least since 1969, been a cheerleader for the partition of Palestine into two states. Now, however, I am firmly convinced that it will not work and that the hopes pinned on it are delusional. When Arafat and his associates came back to the area in 1995 to lead the newly established Palestinian Authority, the deal that was never written down but was always fundamental to the new arrangement was that the Palestinian Authority would control all of the splinter groups that remained at war with Israel and wanted only to destroy it. The war between Israel and the Palestinians has become fiercer because this is precisely what the Palestinian Authority has failed to do, control the armed dissidents.

To be sure, there have been some renunciations by the PLO of the objective enshrined in its national covenant, to eliminate the state of Israel, and there has even been a declaration by the Arab League that Israel would be recognized if certain stringent conditions, including substantial return of Palestinian refugees to areas within Israel's pre-1967 borders, were met—but the makers of the post-Oslo *intifada* have continued to proclaim that they are at war with Israel under all circumstances. Who can grant any kind of reassurance to Israel that a Palestinian state in the West Bank and Gaza trying to establish itself as it also copes with a substantial influx of refugees would be able to keep order and peace? The likelihood is that this could happen only if Israel's armed forces exerted substantial oversight. So, a two-state solution will suffer from looking suspiciously like the situation that obtained before a Palestinian state was announced.

When I have advanced these arguments to some of my friends who pant after a complete, decent, liberal solution to the Palestinian conflict, they have usually answered that a Palestinian state would be led by people who have a stake in its success and survival. Therefore, this state will have to uproot all those living or coming to live in it who want to use it as their base for the struggle with Israel. This is a thesis I cannot believe. Arafat is the perfect proof that it is not so. It is in his self-interest to come to a two-state deal with Israel, but he has recoiled over and over again from negotiating such a deal because he cannot let himself really go to war with the hard-liners among the Palestinians. He seems to know that, at the very least, his own life would be in danger, but, more important still, there would be civil war among the Palestinians. So, the intransigents among the Palestinians still remain in control of policy.

On the Jewish side, the political parties of the extreme right do not even bother hiding their ultimate aim. Much of the time they use a seemingly humane and unbloody term, "transfer," to indicate that Israel should find a way of expelling what remains of its Arab population beyond the Jordan River so that the "undivided land of Israel" would remain entirely in Jewish hands. On less polite occasions, partisans of a completely Jewish state of Israel do not hide their intention to make life so difficult for the Arabs within its borders that they will choose to leave. Such programs simply cannot be realized. Israel could not remain a democratic or a Jewish state and engage in such immoral behavior. In the sixth decade after their defeat in Israel's war of independence, the Palestinian Arabs have proved that they will not go away and that they cannot be driven out. It is simply inconceivable that Israel will ever reach the point of putting at least three million people who reside within its borders or in territory that Israel controls on trucks to drive them to the Jordan River, where they will be forced at bayonet point to ford the shallow stream in the teeth of Jordanian military resistance arrayed on the east bank of the river.

The question, therefore, remains: Is there a way out? If peace cannot be made on any basis that is proposed by any of the parties to the quarrel, is some lessening of the hostilities, some détente, possible? Is it still within the power of the combatants to come up with some workable plan or have they exhausted all the options and are now reduced to ever angrier impotence?

I think all of the combatants' options have been exhausted. I am persuaded, after fifty years of involvement in the problems of the Palestinian-Israeli conflict, that the hope that the two parties can find ways of settling the quarrel between them is a myth that needs to be retired. They never have been able to, not from the very beginning. Other powers have always brokered the arrangements that have stopped hostilities. The only question that remains to be investigated is whether this conflict is sufficiently threatening to the peace of the world that others must now invest in making an end of it. There is no doubt that the Bush administration had no choice but to come to this conclusion. Palestine is not a local backwater. This is where a political and military earthquake of major proportion might take place. The United States, the great conservative power in the world, wedded as it is to order and stability, cannot sit by and let such a disaster happen.

◇◇◇◇◇◇◇◇◇

FIVE

IS A FUTURE POSSIBLE?

N egotiations in the past hundred years have proved, over and over again, that Jews and Arabs are incapable of making peace across table. The partition of Palestine in 1947 was imposed by the United Nations. The return of the Sinai Peninsula to Egypt was arranged in a deal brokered by the United States in 1978 and paid for by American foreign aid. Israel was promised American money to pay for the withdrawal, and Egypt was given a commitment that it would receive about half of the amount of the foreign aid that is given each year to Israel. American soldiers policed the boundary between Israeli and Egyptian military formations. The agreement in Oslo in 1993 was negotiated in great secrecy by Israel and the PLO, but it was ratified and announced at the White House by President Bill Clinton.

It is beyond doubt that only the United States has the power to make Israelis and Palestinians accept policies that neither of them could adopt on their own. Détente can be reached in this quarrel only if the United States takes the lead in forcing Israel to withdraw from the West Bank and

East Jerusalem and in forcing the Arabs (and not only the Palestinian Arabs) both to give up violence and to surrender the illusion that the Arab refugees from the war of 1948–49 will ever come back to Israel within its pre-1967 borders. Israelis and the Palestinians would accept such edicts only if imposition by American power would allow them to disclaim responsibility for these unpalatable results.

ATOMIC BOMBS AND THE MIDDLE EAST

Why should the Americans care to get into this quarrel? I am proposing here not the usual clichés about doing good for the Jews or lessening the misery of the Palestinians or gaining goodwill for the United States in the Arab world. The issue today for the United States is one worrying many people: the spread of weapons of mass destruction in the Middle East. The destruction of Saddam Hussein's government in Iraq makes it very likely that individuals or small groups of his technocrats are now in business for themselves. Those Palestinians who are most bitterly at war with Israel are very likely to be their eager customers. Even a "dirty" atom bomb, that is, a device that would not kill many people but that is easy to make out of readily available materials, could nonetheless set off major terror in the region.

The underlying premise of all too many decades of conventional political thought about the quarrel between the Israelis and the Palestinians must now be declared to be irrelevant (and, need I add, bankrupt). It is no longer true that the long-standing war between these two combatants in the Middle East is most easily compared to the even longer lasting fight between Catholics and Protestants in Northern Ireland. By thinking about Israeli-Palestinian conflict in these terms, those who buy into such a definition are making themselves feel better, but this is the use of a bromide at the expense of truth. By no stretch of the imagination do the killings in Northern Ireland amount to more than the pain and terror of a long-lasting local quarrel. Whoever might be winning at any moment, victory or defeat for either side does not threaten the stability of the world.

But what is happening in the Middle East, right now, is different. This is no longer a squabble between two angry ethnic groups. This war can no longer be taken less seriously than such questions as the control of the major sources of oil or control of the strategic areas in the Middle East. The Israeli-Palestinian quarrel cannot be allowed to continue much longer because it is very likely to explode soon as a threat to world peace.

These reflections have made me rethink the events of somewhat more than a hundred years ago, when Theodor Herzl launched political Zionism at the First Zionist Congress in 1897. This was not the first attempt to start a new Zionism. Herzl was no deeper a thinker about the future of Jews and Judaism than Moses Hess, the contemporary of Karl Marx, who had dubbed him "the Communist Rabbi Moses," or than Leon Pinsker, the Russian Jewish doctor from Odessa who responded to the pogroms in Russia in 1881–82 with a brilliant and clear call for the re-creation of Jewish nationalist existence. So why were these two of little effect? Why was modern Zionism left to be reinvented by Theodor Herzl?

The difference is to be found in the underlying premises of these thinkers. Hess and Pinsker faced and accented the misery of the Jews: Jews are under unrelenting attack in much of the modern world, which had promised them acceptance. One of the bases of Herzl's Zionism was the notion that the Western world needed to settle the Jewish question not primarily to make the Jews happy, but for the sake of society as a whole. The Jews needed to be helped to become less angry and less revolutionary, but not totally or even primarily for their own sake. Society as a whole would be better off if Jews stopped knocking, restlessly, on all the doors of the West; let them finally go home to a land of their own and, preferably, to their own land. Herzl was thus transforming the Jewish question from a parochial problem for the Jews into a problem for the rulers of the world. In this grandiose task Herzl succeeded. Everyone was willing to talk with him, including the pope and the sultan in Istanbul, because the hundreds of thousands of Jews on the move and the millions who were angry with their rulers were a matter of the widest concern. The powers of the world could see in the restless Jews the seeds of social turmoil in their own societies. Herzl had made the point unmistakably; he had internationalized the Jewish question.

A similar moment is arriving now, in a far different time. Those who deal with closely guarded information or knowledgeable guesses about the spread of nuclear material have been paying increasing attention to the Israel-Palestine quarrel. There is no large consensus in these circles, but one widely accepted judgment about nuclear spread does exist. Governments, even rogue governments, will not sell or provide nuclear material to any of the revolutionary movements because they are afraid that nuclear material sold to some buyer whom they cannot control might soon be used against themselves. The continuing fear is that private enterprise might provide the atomic material or, for that matter, the chemical and biological weapons that governments will not sell or give away. To be sure, the Russian government is guarding ten thousand existing atomic bombs, and it has signed a treaty in which it has sworn not to sell or give away any nuclear material, but this watch is not foolproof. Rumors keep multiplying that some of this material has been finding its way into international black markets, where it can be acquired by any who can pay.

These fears have become greater recently with the fall of Saddam Hussein in Iraq. We do not yet know what weapons of mass destruction he had created and where they might be, but it is abundantly clear that there are a large number of trained technocrats without jobs who are now doing the best they can to create connections for themselves. We have no clue about what they might be bringing with them in the way of material, but it is beyond doubt that the expertise exists among them to do great harm. It does not take a large stretch of the imagination to see a few of them working in some hidden bomb factory much closer to Tel Aviv and West Jerusalem than Baghdad.

Even before the newest convulsion in the region, the takeover by the United States and its allies of Iraq, the fear was already growing that the weapons with which the Palestinian militants were arming themselves were becoming more sophisticated. There were rumors that some of the bomb factories hidden in the West Bank and Gaza could be manufacturing weapons far more dangerous than the explosive harnesses laden with shrapnel that the suicide bombers detonate at a bus stop or inside a crowded café in Israel.

Some observers with sensibilities sharpened (or oversharpened) from many decades of living with the war between Israelis and Palestinians saw some sign of this growing fear in the radical change in Israeli military tactics in the first few months of 2003. Preventive attacks by the Israeli army were aimed at houses or cellars in apartment houses or public buildings in refugee camps where Israel's intelligence services had reason to believe that bomb factories existed. It was particularly revealing that the Americans made no attempt to restrain the Israelis as they broadened the war. Washington paid little attention to the outcries by the Arabs that Israel had turned "brutalitarian." Supposedly, the Bush government was in ideological alliance with Prime Minister Sharon of Israel, so he was given a blank check, but there is much missing from this explanation.

Even when most indulgent with Sharon, Bush never gave up his support for the peace plan, written by the quartet of the United States, the Soviet Union, the United Nations, and the European Union, that affirmed both support for a Palestinian state and the demand for the end of all new Israeli settlements in the occupied territories (even under the guise of allowing for their "natural growth"), including the dismantling of all settlements that had been established since mid-2001. Bush and Sharon do not agree on the political result that each wants—so why the "blank check" for the Israeli army? It is a reasonable guess that the Americans and the Israelis agreed that the hunt for weapons of mass destruction, the very concern that had taken the Americans, the British, and the coalition they assembled to war in Iraq was being pursued by Israel with quiet approval by, and even encouragement from, Washington. The spread of weapons of mass destruction toward Israel, through the homes, cities, and camps of the Palestinians, was considered to be ever more likely and more dangerous.

The conclusion that flows all too naturally from these considerations is frightening: the question is no longer whether weapons of mass destruction will appear in the conflict between Palestinians and Israelis; it is only a question of how soon. I have not reached this somber conclusion all by myself. Several people who have expert knowledge of the spread of such weapons to the lands nearest the eastern shore of the Mediterranean voiced such conclusions in separate, independent conversations; at no time did I tell any individual what the others had said to me. Their common theme was that a dirty bomb did not require the sophisticated material that could only be bought from smugglers connected to atomic factories or biological and chemical laboratories. A dirty bomb could be put together from material that was readily available at stores that openly sold the ingredients. It is no great feat, I was told several times, to assemble such a bomb.

The technocrats and expert observers with whom I spoke were surprised that it had not yet been done. They added a political consideration: organized states would not engage in such provocation because Israel would surely respond in force, but such restraint does not apply to guerrilla warriors or those they train to be suicide bombers, because they are too dispersed and they are not controlled, at least not completely, by the central governance of their terrorist movements. Those who told me all this sounded clinical and matter-of-fact. I listened to them, and inevitably I thought about my nieces and nephews in Israel and their families and about my friends on both sides of this quarrel. I tried to disguise the fact that my hands kept turning cold and shaking.

How can we avoid the tragedies that seem to be on their way—and quite soon? We have no choice: Israelis and Palestinians will have to swallow bitter pills—yes, they will have to be forced to swallow bitter pills—that they have repeatedly insisted are repulsive.

I must begin with a conclusion about the short run that runs counter to all that I have thought for most of my life. No amount of incantation about the need for Jews and Arabs to turn to the ways of peace can hide the brutal fact that the veto to any peace efforts is in the hands of a minority of intransigents. There is no immediate alternative to the use of force. Israel cannot allow—indeed, it does not have the moral right to allow—its civilian population to be the object of random murder. To be sure, Israel's policy of creeping annexation of Palestinian land makes the situation worse between the two peoples. It is not only up to Israel's own citizens to put an end to this policy. The creeping annexation of the West Bank is also a problem for America, for Israel's actions are an obstacle to any settlement between Jews and Palestinians. Nonetheless, the citizens of the Jewish state cannot be asked to continue in a situation in which Palestinians have free rein to blow up anything or anyone they choose. I know that those with whom I have worked for many years in the peace movement will be surprised that I do not repeat the old rhetoric of the need for peace and understanding. I cannot in good conscience offer this as a solution while everyone in Israel is in direct, immediate, and personal danger of being killed by a sniper or suicide bomber. And everyone in Palestinian lands is in equal danger of being killed in some reprisal raid.

But clearly this is no long-run solution. Military might can put an uprising down and force a lower profile, but every time a refugee camp is invaded by Israeli tanks or a house blown up even if everyone knows that its cellar housed a bomb factory, the Palestinians who have suffered this defeat are angrier than they were earlier that day and more of them are made into likely recruits for the war against Israel. The question then is whether the Israeli use of force to decrease the number of murders is the preamble to a longer and more hostile war or whether it can be transformed into a new approach for peace. Is the present American position in the Middle East an opportunity for a grand settlement?

The unequivocal answer is no. The most recent plan bearing an American imprimatur, the road map devised by the quartet mentioned above (the United States, Russia, the European Union, and the United Nations), has little chance of achieving its announced purpose of bringing a permanent settlement within the next several years. From the Israelis there is much defiance of the suggestion that the continuing annexations in the West Bank be ended. Never mind the acceptance of the road map by the Palestinians:

they are not likely to control Hamas, the Hezbollah, and any other militants who have refused to end their assaults on Israel. Since these are the basic conditions each side must fulfill to make peace negotiation possible, we are being treated to some more of the "theater of the peace process," that is, of talk about peace without much hope of attaining it. Every time I contemplate the wearying succession of peace negotiations between Israel and the Palestinians, I am reminded of a line in T. S. Eliot's poem "The Love Song of J. Alfred Prufrock": "in the room the women come and go, talking of Michelangelo."

CAN THE UNITED STATES BE THE GLOBAL SHERIFF?

But peace is not possible in this quarrel, at least not in our generation, for far deeper and more fundamental reasons than the deadly games that the Palestinians and the Israelis have been playing with each other. The only sheriff in the global village with the power to enforce the law is the government in Washington, but there is overwhelming reason to believe that Washington is not ready to perform such a function. Never mind that the favorite rhetoric of many pundits has now shifted to imagining an American raj stretching from Afghanistan through Iraq to Syria, Lebanon, and Israel/Palestine. Such a new American empire would dominate the oil states, intimidate Iran into obedience, and inevitably carry along Egypt and Jordan.

The trouble with this grandiose scheme is that it is not

consonant with the basic American character. We are essentially an optimistic people. We think that problems can be solved quickly. We do not have the temperament for occupying indefinitely, perhaps for a century or so, large stretches of foreign land, with their civil wars, tribal loyalties, and hatred of the Western foreigners. We walked away from Korea and accepted a stalemate. We accepted defeat in Vietnam. In both cases, the basic reason was that there was no quick solution, and the people of the United States could not face the prospect of receiving thousands of body bags from the other side of the world year by year, for decades.

Let us examine the language of the road map. The authors of this largely American text forecast peace, a final settlement after a century of conflict, in the Israeli-Palestinian war. And then, the peace brokers can go home, having settled the question between the combatants. They can rest and then turn their attention to more pleasant matters. This vision is very American. We have no patience for an unsettled and often unpleasant long run. The United States will not agree to become the long-standing power policing this volatile region from Afghanistan to the Mediterranean.

Equally important is that this notion runs counter to what we know about the region. Most of the essentially Muslim states are not states at all. They are collections of people whose primary loyalties are usually to their tribes or families. They have very little sense of belonging to a national community. Their larger identity is Arab or Muslim, not Iraqi or Afghani or even Palestinian. If the United States ever agrees to become the reigning power in the region, its proconsuls and military will not have safe lives. The local rulers who will govern, supposedly protected by the Americans, will not have the security of believing that they would live long and peacefully, dying in their beds as respected leaders of their people. The most that one can hope for is that the Americans will define their role much more modestly. They will effect those changes that will serve their interests without embroiling themselves in all of the woes of the region.

The logic of what I am saying applies with particular force to the more sophisticated version of the present vision of the Americans as the new raj. It was dressed up some years ago by Shimon Peres, Israel's most durable and prominent statesman, in the notion that the Jewish state and the Arab state should become part of a regional economic and political union in the image of the European Union, in which borders and tariffs have essentially disappeared and nations with long histories of war between each other are now cooperating, more or less as friends. This dream has been revived by President George W. Bush, who is trying to tempt the Arabs to a more peaceful life by offering them the economic enticement of free trade with the United States. Both Peres and Bush are clearly thinking in terms of globalization, that great current mantra of those who would build a more glorious world for the future.

The trouble with globalization is that it is not very popular now in most of the Third World and among much of Western opinion. In the Third World, the drive toward globalization is perceived as the relentless effort to obliterate weaker societies and economies in order to extend the global economic rule by the most powerful elements in the West at the expense of innumerable local interests. In this connection I am reminded of the plea by the first generation of Zionists that they were bringing advanced forms of economic life to the backward land of Palestine. They expected to be welcomed by the Palestinians. They were offering themselves as a vanguard to lead the Arabs of Palestine into the blessings of an advanced society—but the Arabs seemed to prefer, at least a good bit of the time, to shoot to defend their backward ways. Their ways might be backward, but they were their own. Something like this is happening before our eyes these days in Afghanistan, where the tribal warlords prefer to resist reorganization into a cohesive state under American aegis, and in Iraq, where the Americans are having great difficulty leading this conquered country to some form of Western democracy.

Fifty years ago, after the end of World War II, when Western attention was fixed on remaking the world, a popular song suddenly appeared on radios all over the United States. A supposed native of Africa was singing: "Bongo, bongo, bongo, I don't want to leave the Congo." This was about the time that Mahatma Gandhi was assassinated by nationalist fanatics who were furious at his refusal to hate the Muslims, who were then establishing their own state of Pakistan. Gandhi had led India to independence by taking off his striped trousers and morning jacket, the garb of a British lawyer, and putting on a handwoven linen sheet, the cloth with which a simple Indian had covered himself since the preindustrial age. Raymond Aron, a Franco-Jewish political thinker of the middle of the past century, understood this point well when he observed that, given the choice between their faith and the promise of economic advantage, people will almost always choose their faith. I cannot believe that the United States will have the patience to deal with all of the many ethnicities, religious sects, and tribalisms that will oppose the creation of a common market or of globalism.

In the conflict between the Israelis and the Palestinians, it can certainly be proved that each of the parties is acting against its own rational interests. The creeping annexation of the West Bank has been and remains a far more expensive venture than has ever been confronted in all its costs. Israel has allocated resources in the many hundreds of millions to subsidize the increase of settlements and to pay for their defense, but this is only the beginning of the accounting. The efforts and resources that have been spent on these settlements could have assured the demographic future of the Galilee, the region in northern Israel that shares a border with Lebanon. The population figures for the Galilee have, on occasion, been dressed up for political purposes, but there is little doubt that the Jewish majority in that region is very tenuous. Nevertheless, no Israeli government has ever made a serious attempt to strengthen the Jewish presence in that sensitive region.

For that matter, since the founding of the state of Israel in 1948, its indigenous Arab population has grown from something over one hundred thousand to something over one million; that is, more than a million Arabs live inside the green line and are citizens of Israel. Even the most casual drive through the Arab cities and towns of Israel or of Arab East Jerusalem, which Israel annexed, makes one point unmistakably. In the Israeli national budget, Arabs receive services (garbage removal, sanitation, education, etc.) in the amount of perhaps twenty percent of that spent every year on Jewish citizens. It is remarkable that these Arab Israelis have been as law-abiding as they are, for their neglect by Israel is an open wound and an invitation to disaffection. The money that has been spent on settlements in the West Bank or on an embattled enclave in Hebron would have done Israel much more good had it been used to better the lives of the Arabs of Nazareth and East Jerusalem.

The most fundamental issue connected with these settlements is very seldom discussed: their political cost. Soon after the Six-Day War in 1967, Israel established paramilitary settlements to control the Jordan Valley and created some presence on the hills that dominated the center of the West Bank. The reason given for these changes in the landscape was that they were necessary for Israel's defense against the possibility of infiltration or, worse still, frontal attack from the east side of the Jordan River. I did not believe this account because I knew that an important minority in Israel had an entirely different purpose: to occupy the entire biblical land of Israel. Without a doubt, the many dozens of settlements that have been planted in the past few years in the center of the West Bank have not been created in order to help defend Israel. On the contrary, many of these outposts are so exposed that they need defending themselves, and thus they eat up energy, people, and money from the budget of the Israel Defense Forces.

Israel does not often talk about what the settlements cost the state, because it would then have to produce an account for Washington, in which the annual amount of foreign aid is calculated, and the United States might reduce the annual amount of foreign aid that Israel receives, and for New York, where the organizational Jewish leadership has to persuade itself and its constituents that Israel's policies on the West Bank do not drain away any part of American support. Nonetheless, the fear is never quite absent that such an accounting might have to be made. It was once attempted during the regime of the first President Bush. It resulted in a temporary reduction in American aid by the amount being spent on settlements. The government in Washington certainly has the power to make Israel curtail and end settlement activities. No Israeli government could defy such an American demand. Israel would fear that American foreign aid and Washington's automatic veto of attacks on Israel in the United Nations would be affected by such defiance. The United States does not have to involve itself in long-run, elaborate schemes of quasi-trusteeship in this volatile region. All that it needs to do is to stop the settlement activities—and that it can do.

The United States cannot issue such an edict without being equally and uncompromisingly tough with the Palestinians and especially with their hinterland in the Arab world. Here too it must be made very clear that it is against America's interest to put up any further with this warfare. The obvious reason is that it is turning more and more dangerous; the level of violence is on the verge of escalating.

As long as the war against Israel can be portrayed as the central issue uniting the Arab world, two processes seem unstoppable. One is that the United States, as the principal supporter of Israel on the international scene, is portrayed as part of an unholy anti-Arab alliance. More subtly and insidiously, this pseudounity around the anger of the Palestinians allows the Arab world to direct its attention away from its own internal problems. The street is disaffected or even revolutionary in almost every country, so it is better for the various autocracies to encourage their enemies in the street to demonstrate against Israel than against their own rulers.

Indeed, this game is reminiscent of the one that czarist Russia played in the last half century before the Revolution of 1917: better to let the angry mobs make pogroms against the Jews so they would forget their anger at the czar. The variation of this situation in the current Arab scene goes like this. Everyone knows that free elections in most Arab nations would result in the installation of a revolutionary anti-American regime. One can almost hear the private conversations in which discreet emissaries from Arab governments and the PLO tell policymakers in Washington that it is best to let the angry militants demonstrate against the Zionist Jews and even burn Israeli and American flags than to put a stop to the practice. The street might then discover its real woes: poverty, corrupt rulers, and the lack of hope that their societies will ever provide for their future.

It is clear that in its own interest the United States needs more reasonable politics in the Middle East, and especially in the Israel/Palestine quarrel. Most immediately, the United States and all the powers involved in the region need an end to the threat posed by weapons of mass destruction. But there is a long and difficult distance between wanting nuclear disarmament and the disappearance of all other weapons of mass destruction from the western Mediterranean and actually achieving this result. How, indeed, can the United States and its principal ally, Great Britain, move effectively to control the weapons that might be pouring into Israel/Palestine? The one thing that the United States cannot and should not do is to engage this problem directly on the ground. American intelligence will certainly not be more effective than Israeli intelligence in finding out who the potential suicide bombers may be and what targets they have selected.

We must not urge the Americans to join the Israelis in policing the West Bank and Gaza or to impose an American trusteeship on the Palestinian areas. This would not end the violence. On the contrary, it would trap the United States in a cat-and-mouse game with the Arab militants. It would make American soldiers into the targets of attack. Direct American control is likely to dismay and enrage the Israelis, who would claim, at least some of the time, that the Americans are letting the Palestinian gunmen and suicide bombers off too lightly. Let us not forget that direct American participation in repressing the Palestinian militants would embarrass and upset Israel's friends, especially Jews, in the United States. The last thing they would want to hear is enemies of Israel chanting on the streets before television cameras that American boys and girls are being put in harm's way to defend the interests of the Jews. But the United States can and must do what is in its own interest: to stop the flow of weapons of mass destruction everywhere, especially into Israel/Palestine.

In another war the United States has been fighting in recent years, the battle against drugs, we have moved away from the notion that we can control this traffic by finding the consumers of the drugs or the small pushers who supply them. The only way to make a real dent in this trade is to find the fields in which the drugs are grown and the factories in which the drugs are refined from plants. By the same token, we can control weapons of mass destruction only if we find the underground sources of production and distribution. My friends among those who watch this traffic keep insisting that their major worry is not in what India or Pakistan or even Iran might be producing and selling, at least in small quantities. The main worry remains the huge arsenal of the Soviet Union. No one seems to be able to produce proof, at least on the record, that terrorists in the Middle East can and will acquire weapons of mass destruction from Russia, but that premise has seemed implicit in all the conversations I have had with people who have devoted their lives to studying this threat.

The United States does give some money to the government of Russia to improve its guard against theft and to pay for the dismantling of atomic arms, but what the Russians are doing, even with our help, is simply not enough. The control of the atomic material that has been stockpiled from the dismantled arms is not adequate, especially since we know that Russia's atomic workers are now poorly paid and many are out of jobs. If the international leakage of fissionable material is to be stopped, the United States must help Russia do much more to provide decent jobs for these prime losers at the end of the Cold War, the men and women of Russia's atomic industry.

How strange it is that the modern Zionist community in Palestine came in the beginning from Russia. Now, the safety of the world as a whole requires that Russia be put out of business as a possible major source of atomic instability. Israel will, incidentally, be made safer, but this will happen as part of the global endeavor to control the illicit spread of weapons of mass destruction. How odd that an inkling of this thought was written in the Talmud nearly two thousand years ago: "Every difficult problem that attaches itself only to the Jews is not a problem; a true problem is one in which Jews and all the rest of the world are equally affected."

WHAT FORCE SHOULD THE UNITED STATES USE?

Is it within American power to calm down the Israeli/Palestinian conflict? The United States does have the means with which to impose its will, but, as I have been insisting, we must put limits on what we should, and should not, do. Our government should not put troops on the ground to hound those who send suicide bombers into Israel or to stop the building of more Jewish settlements in the West Bank, for we would be playing the thankless role of the British in the 1930s and 1940s as the conflict between the Jews and the Palestinians became ever bloodier. But we can force a reduction of the violence on both sides.

A first principle of economics is that money is fungible. The United States finances about four billion dollars a year, on average, of Israel's national budget. The continuing effort to support and increase settlements in the West Bank and Gaza costs at least a billion dollars a year. The money spent outright as subvention of the settlements was estimated most recently, in the year 2001, as amounting to some four hundred million dollars a year, but there is also the cost of defending these settlements and of absolving them and their inhabitants of much of Israeli taxation. An American government that resolved to stop the settlements would not need to keep sending the secretary of state and other emissaries again and again to Jerusalem to say to the Israeli administration that we really mean what we say. We could prove it by deducting the total cost of the settlements each year from America's annual allocation to Israel. To prove that we were not being unfeelingly mean, the American administration should add that it would hold a billion dollars a year in escrow with which to help those of the settlers (the polls tell us that they would be more than half of their number) who would peacefully move back into Israel's pre-1967 borders.

No doubt there would be an outcry among the right-wing supporters of Israel who want to realize the ultra-nationalist vision of the undivided land of Israel. But an American government that would have the courage to force the end of settlement activity would find far greater support in the Jewish community both in Israel and in America than many of the people in Washington imagine.

It is beyond doubt that in Israel the majority knows that the creeping annexation of the West Bank must be stopped. In the Jewish world as a whole, the forcing of the end of almost all of the settlements is an appealing idea. It is much more popular than it appears to be in the statements by the pro-Israel lobbying establishments in America. Underneath the noises of these maximalists, there is a worried majority Jewish opinion about the demographic picture in the undivided land of Israel. Between the Mediterranean and the Jordan River, the total population is now more than 40 percent Arab. As is well known, the Arab birthrate is far higher than the Jewish (more than two to one), so there will be an Arab majority in at most twenty years. At that point Israel will effectively be a binational state. It will have to make a fateful choice between being a democracy that will empower the Arab majority to dominate its government or to subject the Palestinian Arabs to a rule reminiscent of South Africa before the age of Nelson Mandela.

The hard-liners in Israel and their supporters abroad avoid this prospect by talking about transfer of population or of making life so difficult that the Palestinians would choose to leave. This is nonsense. Life has been difficult for the Palestinians for several decades, but they have not gone away in large numbers. The other hope of the hard-liners is that the messiah will come and therefore the Jews will not in this fabled "end of days" have to pay any political bills that they have incurred by seeding the West Bank with ever more settlements. But the messiah seems to have a very bad habit of not showing up when we think he ought. He did not appear in front of the gas chambers in Auschwitz in 1943.

The mainstream in Israel and in the Jewish Diaspora will be grateful to America for saving it from itself. The American government must act with comparable tough love toward the Palestinians. It may take a little longer, but here too an American initiative will be greeted with large relief.

There is growing awareness among many Palestinians that they cannot win their war with Israel and that they dare not wait for their militants to go nuclear, for the likely Israeli response would be fierce. It would make an end of Palestinian hopes for a long, long time.

But the United States cannot replace Israel in policing the territories, for that task might become endless. What American influence can achieve—and it must—is to dry up the financial and military support of the Palestinian warmakers. It is within our power to freeze their financial accounts in many countries and to insist that both our allies and, bluntly speaking, those who fear us, such as the Syrians, cease supplying the most violent Palestinian factions with war material.

The Iranians and the Saudis are known to be the largest suppliers of money to the most violent faction, Hamas. The Iranian government admits to giving Hamas three million dollars a year, but a recent estimate by the Council on Foreign Relations is that the figure is probably thirty million. Saudi Arabia has been providing many millions through foundations that give for the supposedly charitable work of Hamas in support of its schools and hospitals. The Saudi contributions have government blessing through the Minister of Interior, Emir Naef, who is the president of one of the most important of these supposedly charitable bodies, the "Saudi Committee for Support of Intifada al Quds." A wide network of such charities exists in the United States (where several have been outlawed) and in England, France, Germany, and a variety of other countries. The rationale for this financial support is that none of the money is used to finance Hamas's terrorist activities, but this has been proved untrue. Those who are giving the money know very well that some of it pays for Hamas's military activities. There is now ample evidence in documents that the Israelis found in an incursion into Tulkarm, an Arab town in the West Bank, that Saudi funds were transmitted with clear knowledge that the fighting units of Hamas were being financed.

The sources of supply of arms and munitions are just as varied. The government of Belarus is known to be acquiring hard currency in hundreds of millions by supplying Palestinian customers. In January 2002 the Israeli navy captured a ship that was loaded with a hundred million dollars worth of forbidden war material. This ship was on its way from Iran and its cargo had been ordered and paid for by the Palestinian Authority. It is clear, as President Bush and his administration have agreed, that Hamas, and all the Palestinian terrorists, must be disarmed. This can happen only if the United States makes it absolutely clear to a whole host of countries, including some of our Western allies, whose hands are not clean, that continuing to supply the Palestinians with arms that they should not have would be regarded by the United States as an act of aggression.

But we must also be holding out some hope to the Palestinians. As we impound the banking accounts of the charities that are supposedly helping them, we must not let these funds languish. Whatever authority is created to use this money must also become the sole address for the contributions that Saudi and other supposedly pure charities want to contribute to the region. Let the United States, and those of its allies who will want to join this effort, become the authority that finances schools for the young that will educate them for useful lives but keep out of the curriculum the glorification of suicide bombers. We should use this money, including the hundreds of millions that the Arafat regime has kept hidden from view and has never accounted for, to pay for higher education and investments in new enterprises that will open doors to jobs. The task of the United States in Palestine is to give this troubled and angry people some hope.

No doubt there will be a huge outcry, but in the end the protests against these tough measures will fade. The Israelis will know that we are saving the Jewish state. It will be widely recognized among the Palestinians that we are helping them with their real problem: how to find work and living wages in a region that is now economically depressed. At that point, the Israelis and Palestinians will have a common cause, to find ways of helping each other to wage peace.

A "grand settlement" is not in sight, but the United States can lead both parties to more livable, unideological accommodations. When the Israelis and the Palestinians are left to settle the problems between them, they will be forced to make major decisions. The Israelis will have to choose whether they belong to the West or whether they intend to settle into the Arab Middle East. Much rhetoric has already been devoted to this grand question. From the very beginnings of modern Zionism those who were coming to the land of Israel were regaled with stories about themselves as an Oriental tribe returning to the home and culture of its ancestors. Countering this romantic notion was the hard truth that a majority of Jews had lived for so long in the European West that the culture, habits, and political and economic archetypes they were bringing with them belonged to the European world. To be sure, this westernization was not admired by most Arabs; on the contrary, it allowed many of their writers and intellectuals to deride the Jews as coming to create a Jewish state that would be just as foreign as the kingdom that the Crusaders had established in the twelfth century. The Arabs did not hide their hope that the Jewish state would be as short-lived as the Crusader kingdom.

Some Israelis today rue the fact that Arab language and culture have not been taught effectively in the Jewish schools in Israel. More should be done, but any informed observer of Israel knows beyond any shadow of a doubt that the decision has long been made. Israel regards itself as a European, Western country and perhaps even as the "fifty-first state" of the American union. It is possible that Israel would choose to continue to have deep ties with the Palestinian economy and to derive much of its labor force from among the Palestinians, but this is far from certain. There is a strong tendency now to secure the physical safety of Israel by excluding Palestinian workers. If Israel does erect a fence between itself and Palestinian territory, it will have made its choice. The Israelis might hedge their bets by leaving some doors open for economic cooperation with the Palestinians, but this will not happen for ideological reasons—it will represent the acceptance of economic need—but the fundamental undertow of Israel's direction will have to be toward the West. Israel's economy is already deeply linked with the world of contemporary high tech, and its culture is Western, from its universities to its pubs and bars to its popular culture and even to its religious extremists, who have much more in common with some of the religious currents in Europe and America than they have with the extremists in the Muslim world.

Once substantial peace and personal security exist again for both Israelis and Palestinians, it will be possible to think about the future. The Palestinians cannot be left in misery in refugee camps. The next generation or two must be trained to take an active role in a modern economy. In the first years some of the donors might regret the effort. The first fruits of such education are often young people who bring their rage at the deprivations of their childhood into the schools in which they are being trained for a better day. Nonetheless, there is no alternative to bringing the Palestinians into the conventional life of the contemporary economy. When Israelis and Palestinians finally meet each other as cultural and economic equals, it will become possible to sketch out some lasting political arrangements, perhaps even a two-state solution, for each side will have a stake of its own to safeguard.

No less than the Israelis, the Palestinians will learn to defend their own identity from secular sources. To be sure, ideologically and emotionally the Palestinians will want to think of themselves as part of the Arab Muslim world, but they will be looking at the major actors in that world with profound disappointment. The supposedly powerful Arab states and political leaders will not have saved the Palestinians from disarmament by the Americans and the Israelis. The Arab Muslim world as a whole will have discovered that the West desires no holy war against Islam, but it would not surrender to those who thought that the "great Satan," the United States, would cower before terrorism. Above all, the Palestinians and their supporters will be forced to conclude that the United States will not deliver Israel into their hands. The unconcealed objective of the Arab militants is and remains the destruction of the state of Israel. That objective is beyond the power of the Arab world as a whole. It would certainly be beyond the power of semidisarmed Palestinians to effect so fundamental a change in the pro-Israel orientation of the American government and of a substantial majority of the American people.

In these suggestions I have been insisting that the United States play a decisive, but limited, role in the dealing with the present turmoil in the Middle East. I repeat that it is necessary for everyone's safety that we put a firm lid on terrorism and its most dangerous tool, the spread of weapons of mass destruction, but the United States should not be tempted into the role of the permanent policeman in this part of the world. The United States must defuse the most inflammatory pieces of the Israeli-Palestinian confrontation without remaining on the immediate scene. Why am I so insistent about what appear to be half measures? Why am I not being swept away by the rhetoric of conservative U.S. intellectuals in and out of government (e.g., Donald Rumsfeld and William Kristol, among a host of others) that Washington now has sole hegemony of the world and it should not hesitate to make its imperial wishes known?

Such a policy is likely to be disastrous everywhere, and nowhere more so than in Israel/Palestine. The continuing exercise of unabashed American power and American control in the Muslim world will allow the enemies of the United States to continue their war against the "great Satan" and to use it as their principal concern and source of unity. Inevitably, of course, Israel, even if it is forced to give up its policy of settlements in the West Bank, will continue to be denounced as a partner of the United States. The Arab world will thus be given the opportunity to avoid dealing with itself. It will not have to face the uncomfortable fact that Arab terrorism does not really have the United States as its main enemy. It is really being aimed at the rulers of the Arab world.

The attacks in Saudi Arabia have been assaults on housing projects in which foreigners live, but these installations were guarded by the Saudi government. The success of these assaults means that the ruling princes are not securely in control. This point was already made some years ago when the holiest mosques of Islam, in Mecca, were occupied by armed members of a dissident religious sect. The Saudis have done their best to let the world know as little as possible about this event, but it took a large and bloody struggle for the Saudi government to regain control of these sacred sites. The message seems finally to be getting through to the Saudis that a large number of the terrorists were born, raised, and educated within their kingdom; much of the money supporting them comes from Saudi sources and even from elements within its government.

Among the Palestinians, people are becoming aware of the corruption of many of the leaders of the Palestinian Authority, including Yasir Arafat himself (who is reliably reported to control many, many millions for which he accounts to no one). Questions are being asked about whether the lack of a more believable Palestinian society, one based on law rather than a system of personal cliques and bribery, is a major cause of the misery in which they are living. These questions will not come to the fore among the Palestinians as long as the obvious insult to and assault on their lives by creeping dispossession from the West Bank and Gaza is at the center of their concern. But these issues are equally unlikely to surface if the Americans become the long-term minders of the Palestinian lands, to make sure that they "behave themselves." The policy of the United States, and for that matter Israel, has to be based on a simple principle: give the Muslim world, including the Palestinians, enough room to run their lives so that they cannot avoid dealing with their own problems.

At some future time of political sobriety—soon, it is hoped—Palestinians will finally have to ask themselves whether they really want to spend the next several centuries at war with Israel in the hope of eventually destroying it. They might even begin to wonder whether four million Palestinian refugees (and the number keeps growing by natural means) can really survive on memories from their past while they live on the margins of Arab society. For that matter, Israel will have to ask itself what it intends to do with its own deepest problems: how to relate to the Arabs who live in the Jewish state, and how to remain Jewish and be a democracy. Israel will have to square the circle as it continues to insist that Jews from anywhere in the world, no matter how long they might have been estranged from their Jewishness, have an automatic right of return to their homeland, Israel, but Arabs who were born in the land and then fled from it or were pushed out in war cannot claim such a right for themselves. Perhaps even more fundamental to the ultimate character of Israel, it will have to work out the balance between the secular and religious elements within its society. This battle is still obscured somewhat by the need for national unity in the face of the continuing threat to Israel's security, but what will Israel decide when it is no longer under daily attack and is free to face this deep internal rift within its society?

What I have been saying here runs contrary to a very deep current of hope and near religious certainty among those who have been engaged in the peace process, the long-term effort to find a way of bringing the Israeli-Palestinian war to an end. There is so much agreement among the hopeful about an imminent solution that it is difficult, and even seems churlish, to take a stand against the seeming certainty of a solution: two states, the end of violence, and accommodation on all other matters. The dominant version of this hope continues to be the assumption that one more hard push at the negotiating table will bring victory for reason. The less hopeful, on the Israeli side, have lately been envisaging the unilateral withdrawal of Israel from the West Bank and Gaza and, for security, the establishment of a fence, staffed by Israel, on the border between it and the West Bank.

The good effect of such a fence, as Yuval Elizur has argued in a recent essay in *Foreign Affairs* (January 2003), is that it will afford Israel control of Palestinians who wish to enter its territory and would force the Palestinians to turn to the development of their own economy within their own region, which they will be free to transform quickly into an independent state. The trouble with this plan is that there is no guarantee that the fence will be built at or near the old border between Israel and the West Bank. On the contrary, sections that have already been built (by August 2003) cut off tens of thousands of Palestinians from their farms or homes. The only way an international border could be drawn in this volatile region is if it has more legitimacy than can be imposed by Israel's unilateral will. A boundary between an Israeli and a Palestinian state can exist soon only by international imposition. It would be best if there were a first step: forbidding Israel to eat up more of the West Bank through its settlements in the region and stopping the access of the Palestinians to the most dangerous of weapons.

Almost two centuries ago, Talleyrand, the diplomat and politician who survived all the changes in regime in France during and after the revolution, is reputed to have said to a young man whom he was sending out to a foreign country as ambassador: "Above all, don't be too zealous." My translation of the meaning of this dictum for the present turmoil in the Middle East is to say to the Americans: reduce the dangers that these problems pose, but do not become zealots who are persuaded that they can and must solve them permanently.

We must calm down those who are eager to settle the problems of the world through some mixture of power and angry idealism. We must remember the political wisdom that Sir Isaiah Berlin spent much of his life trying to impart: do not be an absolutist in defense of what you think is virtue, because the defenders of ideals have a habit, in the end, of becoming inquisitors. So, in our journey through the story of the hundred years' war between the Zionists and Arabs, we have found that most of the Palestinians have not yet really budged from their assertion that the Jews stole Palestine from them and that that wrong must be righted. A significant number of Jews keep saying that the messiah will soon come to justify their effort to keep the whole of the biblical land. A third faction, consisting mostly of liberal ideologues in the West, argues that the doctrine of universal rights precludes Jewish nationalism. They must move now toward a calmer and less threatening time. The protagonists must be led or cajoled or even forced to leave behind their religious and ideological assertions to ask: What can we do to make life safer and more decent for Jews and Arabs alike?

EPILOGUE

◇◇◇◇◇◇◇◇◇

In the early 1970s I was invited to a meeting at Harvard Divinity School in which men and women of the several biblical faiths were to discuss a specific question: "What can the religious traditions contribute to making peace between the Israelis and the Palestinians?" I was asked to speak first in the expectation that I would explain the relationship between religious faith and ethnic loyalty in Judaism. Instead, I gave a one-sentence speech. Its text was "The greatest contribution that religion can make to peace between Jews and Arabs is to get out of the equation." There was, of course, a gasp, and so I added a brief comment: Biblical religions are by their very nature absolute. They cannot easily yield anything to each other. Since peace can be made between Israelis and Palestinians only by compromise, it will happen only when men and women of religion are left outside the door and practical politicians make the necessary untidy deals.

I did not know it at the time, at that meeting in the early 1970s, but what I said there is the seed of this book. But this assertion was rooted in a deeper premise I had fashioned at the very beginnings of my thinking about Zionism. I never believed that any version of Zionist ideology offered the Jews a radical, messianic solution to the long-standing misery of being a persecuted minority almost everywhere in the world. I never believed, not even at the height of euphoria in the days when Israel had defended its new state, that the Jews of the diaspora would return en masse to the land of their ancestors. I predicted in the early 1950s, when I was writing my first essays and my first book on Zionism, that some Jews would return to Zion, and others would choose to remain in the diaspora even as they were thrilled for, supported, and identified with those who were rebuilding a homeland for the entire Jewish people.

In my early essays I understood very well why some of the great ideologues who were the founders of modern Zionism saw the return to Zion as the culmination of Jewish history. I never joined this enthusiasm for two reasons. First, I knew the Jews far too well to believe that they would all give up whatever they had achieved, or expected to achieve, in the freer and more secure diasporas and move to Israel. My second and more important reason for doubting Zionist absolutism was rooted in the Jewish religion. I had been taught by my father the Talmudic belief that the messiah would come when we least expected him and only in God's own time. All that we can do is use our human reason and human efforts to solve the immediate problems of our time. Our task is to preserve and deepen the life of the Jews everywhere, to make it possible for our children and grandchildren to go on to the next era.

From its very beginnings, my Zionism was, therefore, not a restatement of the messianic dream of the Jewish religion, but an instrument of survival and of regeneration in a tragic century. These were the purposes that it served throughout the twentieth century, and these are the purposes that Zionism continues to serve. Since its creation in 1948, Israel has received some two million Jewish immigrants on the run from persecution in various places. Only a Jewish state, that is, a society that existed under the law of return (that any Jew could claim the right to live in Israel), would have accepted such an influx, which more than doubled the number of Israel's inhabitants. In the century to come, the Jewish people continue to worry that some parts of it will need or want to move to the national home. The state of Israel is the guarantee that Jews, indeed, will have somewhere to go. The second issue, cultural survival, remains profoundly important. If Israel were no more, the Jews, and world as a whole, would lose the national home in which Jews wrestle on their own terms with the moral and spiritual problems of modern life. Of course, Jews, like all who live in this era, confront the basic question of our time, the question of values. In Israel their search is different; they are not one of several or many minorities. In Israel, Jews are trying to define themselves by the light of their own traditions. Here they are themselves, on their own terms—so they are, at last, just like everybody else.

We Jews have the right to claim the tools for our survival—but we must remember that other peoples have their own needs and agendas. Therefore, the assertions by men and women of the various religious faiths that they, and they alone, have the true path to carrying out what God wants of us frightened me. The notion that God could leave all of the rest of humankind, except for the church or synagogue or mosque to which I belong, in utter darkness, probably to be damned forever, is simply a theological horror. Could a just and merciful God bring so many millions into the world and leave them without light? Yes, there are passages in the Bible, and in the Scriptures that descend from it, that are that fierce, but this is not the only biblical tradition. The one that dominates is the countertradition, that God loves the Philistines and the Ethiopians as much as he loves the descendants of the patriarch Abraham. We are all his children. Indeed, the Scriptures are the record of a resounding triumph of the belief in love and justice for all over the selfishness of one's own ethnicity and the narrowness of one's own faith.

I did not really tell the truth that day at Harvard, some thirty years ago. I did not want, then or now, for biblical religion to absent itself from the strife between the Palestinians and the Israelis. What I wanted was the insistence of hardliners on both sides to end. Let neither side keep invoking its supposed right to attack the other in the delusion that each is doing God's work. Let them hear the deepest teaching of the biblical faith that we are all God's children. We are a family that must find ways of making peace.

The secularism on which I have insisted in this book is not an assault on religion. On the contrary, it is a metaphor for the fundamental assertion of biblical faith, the Golden Rule: Love thy neighbor as thyself. This was translated some two thousand years ago into the parlance of day-to-day life by Hillel, one of the greatest sages of the rabbinic tradition. He taught that what is hateful to you, you should not do to another. We must, each of us, learn to feel within our own skins the woes and the dreams of the other. I pray that this book will make some contribution to turning the hearts of adversaries, of Jews and Arabs, toward each other.

ACKNOWLEDGMENTS

<><><><><><><><><>

Writing acknowledgments is the very last task in sending a manuscript off to be published. It is the happy day when the work is done. It is all the more cause for rejoicing because the author can tell friends, old and new, how grateful he is for their help.

In thinking through the issues in this book, Andrew Apostolou, Alec Grobman, Mark Friedman, Merav Bin-Nun, and my daughters, Linda and Susan Hertzberg, were enormously helpful. They read the preliminary drafts to make sure that what I was trying to say was clear and well defined. These critical readers were joined by Yuval and Judy Elizur, Naomi Levine, and, as always, Edgar Bronfman, all of whom helped me define my basic ideas.

In seeing this book to press, various people in the offices of HarperSanFrancisco were helpful: Terri Leonard, the managing editor, and Julia Roller on the editorial side; Lisa Zuniga, the production editor, who kept me on the straight and narrow as she has before; Ann Moru, the line editor;

Kimberly McCutcheon, the proofreader; Margery Buchanan, the marketing manager; Joseph Rutt, the designer. The most important debt I owe to the staff of HarperSanFrancisco is to Stephen Hanselman, the publisher, who insisted on editing this book himself. He made fundamental contributions to defining the subject and scope of the work. Mark Tauber, associate publisher of HarperSanFrancisco, was an encouraging presence as the project evolved. I am grateful for the technical help of Josh Suskowitz and for the concern and the wisdom of my agent, Sandy Choron.

On the major issues of this book, I was greatly helped by a friend of many years, Ambassador Philip Wilcox, president of the Foundation for Middle East Peace, whose knowledge of the Israeli/Palestinian issues is very nearly unparalleled, and by the long experience and insights that Robert Einhorn, the senior advisor of the International Security Program at the Center for Strategic and International Studies, and Joseph Cirincione, the senior expert on nonproliferation at the Carnegie Endowment for International Peace, generously made available to me. It goes without saying that the conclusions I drew from what I learned from all three of them are my own responsibility.

My most important debts are to the people who have been helping me for years, day after day. Without them, I could not write. Merline Buddo runs the house to make sure that I am as comfortable and as well as I can possibly be. Carol Ivanovski and I have been writing and worrying together about all of my concerns for twenty years. We have a "gentleman's agreement" that we shall continue to write together for years to come. I could not manage without her. As she has done for more than fifty-two years, my wife, Phyllis, has been the first reader and the final critic. She has helped me weather many crises. I pray that, with God's help, we shall be granted the time and the energy to celebrate the completion of the books I have yet to write.

NOTES

❖❖❖❖❖❖❖❖❖

CHAPTER 1

1. Mekhilta, ba-Hodesh, 11, as quoted in *Encyclopedia Judaica* 10:152.

CHAPTER 2

1. Mark Tessler, *A History of the Israeli-Palestinian Conflict* (Bloomington: Indiana University Press, 1994), pp. 127, 155. In 1891, some Palestinian merchants from Jerusalem complained to the Ottoman government in Istanbul that the Jews might dominate the local trade and threaten the interests of the established Arab merchants. Ten years later, some Arab notables in Jerusalem collected signatures for a petition asking that the right of foreigners to buy land be limited. On the question of Jewish-Arab relations in Palestine, the best fairly recent book is Yosef Gorny, *Zionism and the Arabs, 1882–1948: A Study of Ideology* (Oxford: Oxford University Press, 1987). The most important earlier work is

Neville J. Mandel, *The Arabs and Zionism Before World War I* (Berkeley: University of California Press, 1976).

2. British Foreign Office, *Syria and Palestine,* Peace Handbook #60.

3. *Palestine Royal Commission Report,* p. 145. The Palestine Royal Commission is better known as the Peel Commission after its chairman William Robert Wesley, Lord Peel. Its findings will be discussed in greater detail later in this chapter.

4. The British general, Frederick Morgan, was the director of the United Nations Relief and Rehabilitation Agency (UNRRA) for all of the zones of occupation in Germany. He accused the Jews who were fleeing from eastern Europe of being directed by a secret Jewish political organization. He clearly meant the World Zionist Organization. In a public press conference on January 2, 1946, Morgan added that many of these refugees were bringing large amounts of money with them and that they would soon flood Germany.

5. See Yoav Gelber, *Palestine, 1948: War, Escape and the Emergence of the Palestinian Refugee Problem* (Portland, OR: Sussex Academic Press, 2001), p. 48. The classic book on the subject is, by Benny Morris, *The Birth of the Palestinian Refugee Problem, 1947–1949,* Cambridge University Press, 1987. Morris has proved "that a single-cause explanation of the exodus from most areas is untenable. . . . In general, in most cases, the final and decisive precipitant to fight was Haganah, IZL, then LHI or IDF, or the inhabitants' fear of such attack." His concluding chapter, pp. 286–96, is a carefully balanced and instructive summary of the evidence that Morris collected from many sources.

6. See George Antonius, *The Arab Awakening: The Story of the Arab National Movement* (Beirut, Lebanon: Khayat's College Book Cooperative, 1938).

7. The discussion about the increase of Arab population in Palestine—whether it was caused by natural increase or by Arab immigration—is essentially a political argument. The Zionists, especially the hard-liners among them, usually argue that Arab immigration was a major factor and, therefore, there are fewer "real Palestinians" in Palestine. The Palestinians insist that Arab population growth was overwhelmingly caused by natural increase. The most objective studies tend to downplay the significance of Arab immigration in the 1920s and 1930s. Perhaps something over 10 percent but certainly not more than 15 percent of the Arab population was foreign born. See Tessler, *A History of the Israeli-Palestinian Conflict,* p. 211. The case for much larger Arab immigration into Palestine during the 1920s is made in Fred M. Gottheil's article "The Smoking Gun: Arab Immigration into Palestine, 1922–1931," published in the *Middle East Quarterly,* Winter 2003, Volume X: Number 1. Adding legal and illegal immigration together, Gottheil reaches no firm conclusion, but his argument, that increased opportunity attracts migration, tends to support the higher estimation that 15 percent of the Arabs in Palestine by 1948 were foreign born.

8. See especially the last pages of Rashid Khalidi, *Palestinian Identity: The Construction of Modern National Consciousness* (New York: Columbia University Press, 1997), beginning with p. 194.   •

9. Muhammad Y. Muslih, *The Origins of Palestinian Nationalism* (New York: Columbia University Press, 1988), pp. 181–82, 217.

10. Rashid Khalidi, Lisa Anderson, Muhammad Muslih, and Reeva S. Simon, eds., *The Origins of Arab Nationalism* (New York: Columbia University Press, 1991), p. 181.

CHAPTER 3

1. Smith, C. D., *Palestine and the Arab-Israeli Conflict* (New York: St. Martin's Press, 1992), p. 34.

2. Négib Azoury, *Le Réveil de la Nation Arabe*, Introduction (Paris: Librarie Plon, 1905). In this book, Azoury was the first to suggest the creation of an Arab state in the Near East to be taken from the territory of the Ottoman Empire. This was the program for the organization that he chaired, La Ligue de la Patrie Arabe. Part of this program was to fight the Jews who, so Azoury maintained, had begun an effort to claim and control Palestine. Here, Azoury also announced that he was writing a companion analysis, *Le Péril Juif Universel*.

3. For the quotation from the anonymous pamphlet of 1914, see Tessler, *History of the Israeli-Palestinian Conflict*, p. 144. For the diary quotation, see Mandel, *The Arabs and Zionism Before World War I*, pp. 211–12.

4. See Simon H. Rifkind et al., *The Basic Equities of the Palestine Problem* (New York: September 10, 1947; reprint, New York: Arno Press, 1977), pp. 78–79; and Mark Tessler, *A History of the Israeli-Palestinian Conflict* (Bloomington: Indiana University Press, 1994), pp. 151–52.

5. George Antonius, *The Arab Awakening: The Story of the Arab National Movement* (Beirut, Lebanon: Khayat's College Book Cooperative, 1938), pp. 409–12.

6. The text of this historic pamphlet by Judah Leon Magnes is in my book *The Zionist Idea* (Philadelphia: Jewish Publication Society, 1997), pp. 443–49, especially the opening lines of this essay on p. 443.

7. On Nasser's basic attitude toward Israel, see Tessler, *A History of the Israeli-Palestinian Conflict*, p. 391. Soon after Nasser became president of Egypt, he referred to Israel's existence as a "smear" on the entire Arab nation and added that "shame brought on by the battle of 1948" could not be forgotten.

8. Reproduced in Tessler, *A History of the Israeli-Palestinian Conflict*, p. 374.

9. Tessler, *A History of the Israeli-Palestinian Conflict*, p. 286.

10. *Encyclopedia Judaica* 16:431. Chaim Weizmann's conciliatory speech was given in 1925 at the 14th Zionist Conference; see Tessler, *A History of the Israeli-Palestinian Conflict*, p. 181.

11. See my essay "The View from Cairo," in the *New York Review of Books*, July 28, 1980; reprinted in *Jewish Polemics* (New York: Columbia University Press, May 1992), pp. 9–15.

12. *Encyclopedia Judaica* 16:436.

13. As quoted in my essay "Palestine: The Logic of Partition Today," *Columbia University Forum*, 1970, pp. 17–21, especially p. 20.

14. Edward W. Said, *The Question of Palestine* (New York: Random House, 1979), p. 224.

CHAPTER 4

1. On Voltaire, see my *French Enlightenment and the Jews* (New York: Columbia University Press, 1968), pp. 268–313.

2. Pierre-André Taguieff, "L'émergence d'un judéophobie planétaire: islamisme, anti-impérialisme, antisionisme," *Outre-Terre, Revue française de géopolitique* 3 (janvier-mars 2003): 189–226. See especially p. 208 for a description of the demonstration in the Place de la République.

3. Taguieff, "L'émergence d'un judéophobie planétaire," pp. 211–14. More theoretically, Pierre-André Taguieff, *La nouvelle judéophobie* (Paris: Mille et Une Nuits, 2002) is of importance for the connections he makes under the various kinds of "new Jew hatred."

4. Noam Chomsky, *Middle East Illusions* (Lanham, MD: Rowman & Littlefield, 2003), pp. 223–24.

5. Chomsky, *Middle East Illusions,* p. 223.

6. Chomsky, *Middle East Illusions,* p. 32.

7. Chomsky, *Middle East Illusions,* Introduction, pp. 10–11.

8. Edward Said, "What Israel Has Done," in *Al-Ahram Weekly Online,* 18–24 April 2002, p. 4.

BIBLIOGRAPHY

Antonius, George. *The Arab Awakening: The Story of the Arab National Movement.* Beirut, Lebanon: Khayat's College Book Cooperative, 1938.

Azoury, Négib. *Le Réveil de la Nation Arabe.* Paris: Librairie Plon; Plon-Nourrit et Cie, 1905.

Barsky, Robert F. *Noam Chomsky: A Life of Dissent.* Cambridge, MA: MIT Press, 1997.

Carey, Roane, ed. *The New Intifada: Resisting Israel's Apartheid.* Introduction by Noam Chomsky. London: Verso, 2001.

Chomsky, Noam. *Middle East Illusions.* Lanham, MD: Rowman & Littlefield, 2003.

Cirincione, Joseph, with Jon B. Wolfsthal and Miriam Rajkumar. *Deadly Arsenals.* Washington, DC: Carnegie Endowment for International Peace, 2002.

Gelber, Yoav. *Palestine, 1948: War, Escape and the Emergence of the Palestinian Refugee Problem.* Portland, OR: Sussex Academic Press, 2001.

Gorny, Yosef. *Zionism and the Arabs, 1882–1948: A Study of Ideology.* Oxford: Oxford University Press, 1987.

Hertzberg, Arthur. *The Zionist Idea.* Philadelphia: Jewish Publication Society, 1997.

——. *Jewish Polemics.* New York: Columbia University Press, 1992.

——. *The French Enlightenment and the Jews.* New York: Columbia University Press, 1968.

Khalidi, Rashid. *Palestinian Identity: The Construction of Modern National Consciousness.* New York: Columbia University Press, 1997.

Khalidi, Rashid, Lisa Anderson, Muhammad Muslih, and Reeva S. Simon, eds. *The Origins of Arab Nationalism.* New York: Columbia University Press, 1991.

Kimmerling, Baruch, and Joel S. Migdal. *The Palestinian People: A History.* Cambridge, MA: Harvard University Press, 2003.

Mandel, Neville J. *The Arabs and Zionism Before World War I.* Berkeley: University of California Press, 1976.

Morris, Benny. *1948 and After: Israel and the Palestinians.* Oxford, Oxford University Press, 1990.

——. *The Birth of the Palestinian Refugee Problem, 1947–1949.* Cambridge: Cambridge University Press, 1987.

Muslih, Muhammad Y. *The Origins of Palestinian Nationalism.* New York: Columbia University Press, 1988.

Oren, Michael B. *Six Days of War: June 1967 and the Making of the Modern Middle East.* Oxford: Oxford University Press, 2002.

Proceedings of the Washington Institute. 2002 Weinberg Founders Conference, October 4–6, 2002. Washington, DC: Washington Institute for Near East Policy, 2003.

Rifkind, Simon H., et al. *The Basic Equities of the Palestine Problem.* New York, September 10, 1947; reprint, New York: Arno Press, 1977.

Said, Edward W. *The Question of Palestine.* New York: Random House, 1979.

Smith, C. D. *Palestine and the Arab-Israeli Conflict.* New York: St. Martin's Press, 1992.

Taguieff, Pierre-André. "L'émergence d'un judéophobie planétaire: islamisme, anti-impérialisme, antisionisme," *Outre-Terre, Revue française de géopolitique* 3 (janvier-mars 2003): 189–226.

———. *La nouvelle judéophobie.* Paris: Mille et Une Nuits, 2002.

Tessler, Mark. *A History of the Israeli-Palestinian Conflict.* Bloomington: Indiana University Press, 1994.